Ethical Silence

New Kierkegaard Research

Series Editor: Antony Aumann, Northern Michigan University,
and Adam Buben, Leiden University

Advisory Board: John J. Davenport, Fordham University; Rick Anthony Furtak, Colorado College; Sheridan Hough, College of Charleston; Noreen Khawaja, Yale University; Sharon Krishek, Hebrew University of Jerusalem; John Lippitt, University of Notre Dame Australia; Jon Stewart, Slovak Academy of Sciences; Patrick Stokes, Deakin University

New Kierkegaard Research promotes scholarship on all aspects of Kierkegaard's thought and its legacy. The series includes volumes dedicated to the careful exegesis of Kierkegaard's writings, as well as ones that bring his ideas into dialogue with other thinkers. It also serves as an outlet for books drawing inspiration from Kierkegaard to address current questions in philosophy, religion, and other disciplines.

New Kierkegaard Research is pluralistic in nature. It welcomes proposals from scholars approaching Kierkegaard from either analytic or continental philosophical backgrounds, as well as from those adopting historical, contemporary, or comparative frameworks. Emphasis is placed on philosophical engagement with Kierkegaard's ideas, but the series publishes books by authors working in a variety of academic fields.

Recent titles in the series:

Ethical Silence: Kierkegaard on Communication, Education, and Humility, by Sergia Hay

Ethical Silence

Kierkegaard on Communication, Education, and Humility

Sergia Hay

LEXINGTON BOOKS
Lanham • Boulder • New York • London

Published by Lexington Books
An imprint of The Rowman & Littlefield Publishing Group, Inc.
4501 Forbes Boulevard, Suite 200, Lanham, Maryland 20706
www.rowman.com

6 Tinworth Street, London SE11 5AL, United Kingdom

Copyright © 2020 by The Rowman & Littlefield Publishing Group, Inc.

All rights reserved. No part of this book may be reproduced in any form or by any electronic or mechanical means, including information storage and retrieval systems, without written permission from the publisher, except by a reviewer who may quote passages in a review.

British Library Cataloguing in Publication Information Available

Library of Congress Cataloging-in-Publication Data

Names: Hay, Sergia, 1972- author.
Title: Ethical silence : Kierkegaard on communication, education, and humility / Sergia Hay.
Description: Lanham : Lexington Books, 2020. | Series: New Kierkegaard research | Includes bibliographical references and index. | Summary: "This book analyzes Søren Kierkegaard's message about the ethical necessity of silence in the context of our current information age flooded with sound and words. The author investigates the question of how being silent can make us more ethical"-- Provided by publisher.
Identifiers: LCCN 2020029985 (print) | LCCN 2020029986 (ebook) | ISBN 9781793614483 (cloth) | ISBN 9781793614490 (epub) | 9781793614506 (pbk)
Subjects: LCSH: Kierkegaard, Søren, 1813-1855. | Silence.
Classification: LCC B4377 .H39 2020 (print) | LCC B4377 (ebook) | DDC 198/.9--dc23
LC record available at https://lccn.loc.gov/2020029985
LC ebook record available at https://lccn.loc.gov/2020029986

For David and Karen Nasby

Contents

Acknowledgements ix

Sigla for Kierkegaard's Works xi

Introduction 1

1 Silence in Kierkegaard's Stages 5
2 Kierkegaard's Ethics 13
3 Language and Communication 31
4 Silence 49
5 Ethical Silence 61
6 Exemplars of Communication 77

Conclusion: Consequences of Ethical Silence: Teaching, Freedom, and Responsibility 89

Bibliography 99

Index 105

About the Author 109

Acknowledgements

I was first introduced to the international Kierkegaard community at the Howard V. and Edna H. Hong Kierkegaard Library at St. Olaf College when I was a summer fellow right after graduating from Wellesley. For over twenty-five years since then, I have been very fortunate to work with this group of philosophers, theologians, and literary scholars who extend such hospitality, encouragement, and good will. It is a truly singular group working on a truly singular thinker. It would be impossible to thank everyone in this group by name, but it is important to highlight a few: Gordon Marino, Cynthia Wales Lund, Bruce Kirmmse, Vanessa Rumble, Rick Furtak, Marcia Robinson, Begonya Saez Tajafuerce, and Jamie Lorentzen.

I am also grateful for the mentors whose memory I cherish: Howard and Edna Hong, Ruth Anna Putnam, and Ifeanyi Menkiti. I also thank Lydia Goehr for her advising and friendship.

Thank you to my current and former colleagues and students at Pacific Lutheran University, including Pauline Shanks Kaurin and Clay Snell.

Thank you to Jana Hodges-Kluck and Sydney Wedbush at Lexington Books and Antony Aumann and Adam Buben, editors of the New Kierkegaard Research series, for bringing this book into existence.

Finally, thanks to my family—Todd, Aurland, and Eva—for being so wonderful, fun, and joy-inspiring. I love you.

Credits

Kierkegaard, S. *Practice in Christianity*. Edited and translated by Howard V. Hong and Edna H. Hong. Princeton: Princeton University Press, 1991. Reprinted by permission of Postscript, Inc.

Kierkegaard, S. *Søren Kierkegaard's Journals and Papers: Vols. 1–7*. Edited and translated by Howard Hong and Edna Hong, assisted by Gregor Malantschuck. Bloomington: Indiana University Press, vol. 1: 1967; vol. 3 : 1975. Reprinted by permission of Postscript, Inc.

Kierkegaard, S. *Works of Love*. Edited and translated by Howard V. Hong and Edna H. Hong. Princeton: Princeton University Press, 1995. Reprinted by permission of Postscript, Inc.

Kierkegaard, S. *Upbuilding Discourses in Various Spirits*. Edited and translated by Howard V. Hong and Edna H. Hong. Princeton: Princeton University Press, 1993. Reprinted by permission of Postscript, Inc.

Sigla for Kierkegaard's Works

English Translations

References to Kierkegaard's writings in English use the following standard sigla adapted from Mercer University Press's *International Kierkegaard Commentary* series:

BA   *The Book on Adler*, trans. Howard V. Hong and Edna H. Hong (Princeton: Princeton University Press, 1995).

CA   *The Concept of Anxiety*, trans. Reidar Thomte in collaboration with Albert B. Anderson (Princeton, NJ: Princeton University Press, 1980).

CD   *Christian Discourses* and *The Crisis and a Crisis in the Life of an Actress*, trans. Howard V. Hong and Edna H. Hong (Princeton, NJ: Princeton University Press, 1997).

CI   *The Concept of Irony* together with "Notes on Schelling's Berlin Lectures," trans. Howard V. Hong and Edna H. Hong (Princeton: Princeton University Press, 1989).

CUP *Concluding Unscientific Postscript to "Philosophical Fragments,"* 2 vols., trans. Howard V. Hong and Edna H. Hong (Princeton, NJ: Princeton University Press, 1992).

EO 1 *Either/Or: Part I*, trans. Howard V. Hong and Edna H. Hong (Princeton, NJ: Princeton University Press, 1987).

EO 2 *Either/Or: Part II*, trans. Howard V. Hong and Edna H. Hong (Princeton, NJ: Princeton University Press, 1987).

EUD *Eighteen Upbuilding Discourses*, trans. Howard H. Hong and Edna H. Hong (Princeton, NJ: Princeton University Press, 1990).

FSE   *For Self-Examination* and *Judge for Yourself!*, trans. Howard V. Hong and Edna H. Hong (Princeton, NJ: Princeton University Press, 1990).

FT   *Fear and Trembling* and *Repetition*, trans. Howard V. Hong and Edna H. Hong (Princeton: Princeton University Press, 1983).

JC   "Johannes Climacus or De omnibus dubitandum est." See *Philosophical Fragments*.

JFY   *Judge for Yourself!*, See *For Self-Examination*.

JP   *Søren Kierkegaard's Journals and Papers*, 7 vols., ed. and trans. Howard V. Hong and Edna H. Hong, assisted by Gregor Malantschuk (Bloomington and London: Indiana University Press, vol. 1: 1967; vol. 2:1970; vols. 3 and 4:1975; vols. 5-7: 1978).

KJN 1   *Kierkegaard's Journals and Notebooks: Vol. 1, Journals AA-DD*, ed. Niels Jørgen Cappelørn, Alastair Hannay, David Kangas, Bruce H. Kirmmse, George Pattison, Vanessa Rumble, and K. Brian Söderquist (Princeton, NJ: Princeton University Press, 2007

KJN 2   *Kierkegaard's Journals and Notebooks: Vol. 2, Journals EE-KK*, ed. Niels Jørgen Cappelørn, Alastair Hannay, David Kangas, Bruce H. Kirmmse, George Pattison, Vanessa Rumble, and K. Brian Söderquist (Princeton, NJ: Princeton University Press, 2008

KJN 3   *Kierkegaard's Journals and Notebooks: Vol. 3: Notebooks 1-15*, ed. Niels Jørgen Cappelørn, Alastair Hannay, Alastair Hannay, Bruce H. Kirmmse, David Kangas, George Pattison, Vanessa Rumble, and K. Brian Söderquist (Princeton, NJ: Princeton University Press, 2010)

KJN 4   *Kierkegaard's Journals and Notebooks: Vol. 4: Notebooks NB-NB5*, ed. Niels Jørgen Cappelørn, Alastair Hannay, Alastair Hannay, David Kangas, Bruce H. Kirmmse, David Kangas, George Pattison, Joel D.S. Rasmussen, Vanessa Rumble, and K. Brian Söderquist (Princeton, NJ: Princeton University Press, 2011)

KJN 5   *Kierkegaard's Journals and Notebooks: Vol. 5, Journals NB6-NB10*, ed. Niels Jørgen Cappelørn, Alastair Hannay, Alastair Hannay, Bruce H. Kirmmse, Joel D. S. Rasmussen, Vanessa Rumble, and K. Brian Söderquist (Princeton, NJ: Princeton University Press, 2012)

KJN 6   *Kierkegaard's Journals and Notebooks: Vol. 6, Journals NB11-NB14*, ed. Niels Jørgen Cappelørn, Alastair Hannay, Alastair Hannay, Bruce H. Kirmmse, David D. Possen, Joel D. S.

Rasmussen, Vanessa Rumble, and K. Brian Söderquist (Princeton, NJ: Princeton University Press, 2013)

KJN 7   *Kierkegaard's Journals and Notebooks: Vol. 7, Journals NB15-NB20*, ed. Niels Jørgen Cappelørn, Alastair Hannay, Alastair Hannay, Bruce H. Kirmmse, David D. Possen, Joel D. S. Rasmussen, Vanessa Rumble, and K. Brian Söderquist (Princeton, NJ: Princeton University Press, 2014)

KJN 8   *Kierkegaard's Journals and Notebooks: Vol. 8, Journals NB21-NB25*, ed. Niels Jørgen Cappelørn, Alastair Hannay, Alastair Hannay, Bruce H. Kirmmse, David D. Possen, Joel D. S. Rasmussen, and Vanessa Rumble (Princeton, NJ: Princeton University Press, 2015)

KJN 9   *Kierkegaard's Journals and Notebooks: Vol. 9, Journals NB26-NB30*, ed. Niels Jørgen Cappelørn, Alastair Hannay, Alastair Hannay, Bruce H. Kirmmse, David D. Possen, Joel D. S. Rasmussen, and Vanessa Rumble (Princeton, NJ: Princeton University Press, 2017)

LD   Letters and Documents, trans. Hendrik Rosenmeier (Princeton, NJ: Princeton University Press, 1978).

P   *Prefaces* and *Writing Sampler*, trans. Todd W. Nichol (Princeton, NJ: Princeton University Press, 1997).

PC   *Practice in Christianity*, trans. Howard V. Hong and Edna H. Hong (Princeton, NJ: Princeton University Press, 1991).

PF   *Philosophical Fragments* and *Johannes Climacus*, trans. Howard V. Hong and Edna H. Hong (Princeton, NJ: Princeton University Press, 1985).

PV   "The Point of View for My Work as an Author," "The Single Individual," *On My Work as an Author*, and "Armed Neutrality", trans. Howard V. Hong and Edna H. Hong (Princeton, NJ: Princeton University Press, 1998).

SLW   *Stages on Life's Way*, trans. Howard V. Hong and Edna H. Hong (Princeton, NJ: Princeton University Press, 1988).

SUD   *The Sickness unto Death*, trans. Howard V. Hong and Edna Hong (Princeton, NJ: Princeton University Press, 1980).

TDIO   *Three Discourses on Imagined Occasions*, trans. Howard V. Hong and Edna H. Hong (Princeton, NJ: Princeton University Press, 1993).

TM   *"The Moment" and Late Writings*, trans. Howard V. Hong and Edna H. Hong (Princeton NJ: Princeton University Press, 1998).

UDVS *Upbuilding Discourses in Various Spirits*, trans. Howard V. Hong and Edna H. Hong (Princeton, NJ: Princeton University Press, 1993).

WA *Without Authority*, trans. Howard V. Hong and Edna H. Hong (Princeton, NJ: Princeton University Press, 1997).

WL *Works of Love*, trans. Howard V. Hong and Edna H. Hong (Princeton, NJ: Princeton University Press, 1995).

Danish Texts

The corresponding volume and page number in *Søren Kierkegaards Skrifter* (Copenhagen: Gads Forlag) is provided wherever available. For references to the attached volume of commentary for the SKS, a "K" is added before the volume number.

SKS 1 *Af en endnu Levendes Papirer; Om Begrebet Ironi*, ed. Niels Jørgen Cappelørn, Joakim Garff, Johnny Kondrup og Finn Hauberg Mortensen (Copenhagen: Gads, 1997).

SKS 2 *Enten—Eller. Første del*, ed. Niels Jørgen Cappelørn, Joakim Garff, Johnny Kondrup, and Finn Hauberg Mortensen (Copenhagen: Gads, 1997).

SKS 3 *Enten—Eller. Anden del*, ed. Niels Jørgen Cappelørn, Joakim Garff, Johnny Kondrup, and Finn Hauberg Mortensen (Copenhagen: Gads, 1997).

SKS 4 *Gjentagelsen; Frygt og Bæven; Philosophiske Smuler; Begrebet Angest; Forord*, ed. Niels Jørgen Cappelørn, Joakim Garff, Johnny Kondrup, and Finn Hauberg Mortensen (Copenhagen: Gads, 1997).

SKS 5 *Opbyggelige taler, 1843-44; Tre Taler ved tænkte Leiligheder*, ed. Niels Jørgen Cappelørn, Joakim Garff, Jette Knudsen, Johnny Kondrup, and Finn Hauberg Mortensen (Copenhagen: Gads, 1998).

SKS 6 *Stadier paa Livets Vei*, ed. Niels Jørgen Cappelørn, Joakim Garff, Jette Knudsen, Johnny Kondrup, and Finn Hauberg Mortensen (Copenhagen: Gads, 1999).

SKS 7 *Afsluttende uvidenskabelig Efterskrift*, ed. Niels Jørgen Cappelørn, Joakim Garff, Jette Knudsen, and Johnny Kondrup (Copenhagen: Gads, 2002).

SKS 8 *En literair Anmeldelse; Opbyggelige Taler i forskjellig Aand*, ed. Niels Jørgen Cappelørn, Joakim Garff, and Johnny Kondrup (Copenhagen: Gads, 2004).

Sigla for Kierkegaard's Works xv

SKS 9   *Kjerlighedens Gjerninger*, ed. Niels Jørgen Cappelørn, Joakim Garff, and Johnny Kondrup (Copenhagen: Gads, 2004).

SKS 10   *Christelige Taler*, ed. Niels Jørgen Cappelørn, Joakim Garff, and Johnny Kondrup (Copenhagen: Gads, 2004).

SKS 11   *Lilien paa Marken og Fuglen under Himlen; Tvende ethisk-religieuse Smaa-Afhandlinger; Sygdommen til Døden; "Ypperstepræsten"—"Tolderen"—"Synderinden"*, ed. Niels Jørgen Cappelørn, Joakim Garff, Anne Mette Hansen, and Johnny Kondrup (Copenhagen: Gads, 2006).

SKS 12   *Indøvelse i Christendom; En opbyggelig Tale; To Taler ved Altergangen om Fredagen*, ed. Niels Jørgen Cappelørn, Joakim Garff, Anne Mette Hansen, and Johnny Kondrup (Copenhagen: Gads, 2008).

SKS 13   *Dagbladsartikler 1834-48; Om min Forfatter-Virksomhed; Til Selvprøvelse*, ed. Niels Jørgen Cappelørn, Joakim Garff, Johnny Kondrup, Tonny Aagaard Olesen, and Steen Tullberg (Copenhagen: Gads, 2009).

SKS 14   *Bladartikler*, ed. Niels Jørgen Cappelørn, Joakim Garff, Johnny Kondrup, Tonny Aagaard Olesen, and Steen Tullberg (Copenhagen: Gads, 2010).

SKS 15   *Et Øieblik, Hr. Andersen!; Johannes Climacus eller De omnibus dubitandum est; Polemik mod Heiberg; Bogen om Adler*, ed. Niels Jørgen Cappelørn, Joakim Garff, Johnny Kondrup, Tonny Aagaard Olesen, and Steen Tullberg (Copenhagen: Gads, 2012).

SKS 16   *Synspunktet for min Forfatter-Virksomhed; Hr. Phister som Captain Scipio; Den bevæbnede Neutralitet; Dømmer Selv!*, ed. Niels Jørgen Cappelørn, Joakim Garff, Johnny Kondrup, Tonny Aagaard Olesen, and Steen Tullberg (Copenhagen: Gads, 2012).

SKS 17   *Journalerne AA-DD*, ed. Niels Jørgen Cappelørn, Joakim Garff, Jette Knudsen, and Johnny Kondrup (Copenhagen: Gads, 2000).

SKS 18   *Journalerne EE-KK*, ed. Niels Jørgen Cappelørn, Joakim Garff, Jette Knudsen, and Johnny Kondrup (Copenhagen: Gads, 2001).

SKS 19   *Notesbøgerne 1-15*, ed. Niels Jørgen Cappelørn, Joakim Garff, Jette Knudsen, and Johnny Kondrup (Copenhagen: Gads, 2001).

SKS 20   *Journalerne NB-NB5*, ed. Niels Jørgen Cappelørn, Joakim Garff, Jette Knudsen, and Johnny Kondrup (Copenhagen: Gads, 2003).

SKS 21   *Journalerne NB6-NB10*, ed. Niels Jørgen Cappelørn, Joakim Garff, Jette Knudsen, and Johnny Kondrup (Copenhagen: Gads, 2003).

SKS 22	*Journalerne NB11-NB14*, ed. Niels Jørgen Cappelørn, Joakim Garff, Anne Mette Hansen, and Johnny Kondrup (Copenhagen: Gads, 1997).
SKS 23	*Journalerne NB15-NB20*, ed. Niels Jørgen Cappelørn, Joakim Garff, Anne Mette Hansen, and Johnny Kondrup (Copenhagen: Gads, 2007).
SKS 24	*Journalerne NB21-NB25*, ed. Niels Jørgen Cappelørn, Joakim Garff, Anne Mette Hansen, and Johnny Kondrup (Copenhagen: Gads, 2007).
SKS 25	*Journalerne NB26-NB30*, ed. Niels Jørgen Cappelørn, Joakim Garff, Anne Mette Hansen, and Johnny Kondrup (Copenhagen: Gads, 2008).
SKS 26	*Journalerne NB31-NB36*, ed. Niels Jørgen Cappelørn, Joakim Garff, Anne Mette Hansen, and Johnny Kondrup (Copenhagen: Gads, 2009).
SKS 27	*Løse Papirer*, ed. Niels Jørgen Cappelørn, Joakim Garff, Anne Mette Hansen, and Johnny Kondrup (Copenhagen: Gads, 2013).
SKS 28	*Breve og Dedikationer*, ed. Niels Jørgen Cappelørn, Joakim Garff, Anne Mette Hansen, and Johnny Kondrup (Copenhagen: Gads, 2013).

Where the relevant text does not appear in the SKS, reference is made to *Søren Kierkegaards Papirer*, vols. I–XVI, ed. P. A. Heiberg, V. Kuhr, E. Torsting, Niels Thulstrup, and Niel Jørgen Cappelørn (Copenhagen: Gyldendal, 1909–1948; 1968–1970; 1975–1978), designated "*Pap.*" and cited in the conventional format: volume and tome number followed by entry category and number, for example (*Pap.* X–6 B 79). For letters and papers not contained in the SKS or the *Papirer*, reference is made to *Breve og Akstykker vedrørende Søren Kierkegaard*, 2 vols., ed. Niels Thulstrup (Copenhagen: Muksgaard, 1953–1954), designated "A&B" and cited using a volume number followed by a page number.

Introduction

Silence means something different in 2020. The global pandemic of COVID-19 rages as this book is being completed and shrouds the globe with a unique kind of silence, one that is eerie, fear and grief laden, disconnecting, lonely, and disorienting. When we speak with each other, our words are accompanied with respiratory droplets that may or may not contain a fatal virus. Much of our communication now is conducted through technology and gesture—video conferencing, phone, waves, head nods. For those severely impacted by the crisis, there is the anguish of dying alone in silence.

Silence also poses large scale political dangers in a time when democracies, educational institutions, and the free press are threatened. Silence can suppress the truth, house shame, fester fears, excuse the guilty, exclude the disenfranchised, hide all sorts of harms and thereby make the silent one complicit in them. Choosing to be silent is an ethical matter.

Yet, at several different points of his writings, Kierkegaard calls for silence in the form of imperatives. For example:

> ... let us learn *silence*, or learn to be *silent*. (WA 10/SKS 11:16)
> ... create silence! ... Oh, create silence! (FSE 47–8/SKS 13:74–75)

What if the positive ethical aspect of silence is underexplored? How may silence make us better ethically?

In spite of our typical associations of silence with deception and censorship, Kierkegaard's identification of silence with both inwardness and decisive action makes silence critical to his Christian and action-based second ethics. This book builds a case for a Kierkegaardian notion of ethical silence by showing how silence contributes to the fulfillment of the second ethics' imperatives by halting incessant chatter and noise, and setting the "fundamental tone" (FSE 49/SKS 13:75) for ethical activity. Silence's ethical function is specifically in play when we are to refrain from speaking in order to humble ourselves and build up the neighbor. In this way, silence equalizes the self with others by bringing the self's perceived status down and raising the status of the other through love. This book also applies ethical silence to the broader task of interpreting Kierkegaard's views on communication through action, the proper role of educators, and humility.

Earlier investigations of Kierkegaard's views on silence have focused on its connection to the aesthetic and religious spheres, and neglected its connection to the ethical sphere. The scholarship on Kierkegaard's views of silence, for example by Ettore Rocca, Mark Taylor, Wanda Warren Berry, Onno Zijlstra, Steven Shakespeare, Michael Strawser, and Simon Podmore, primarily discuss silence in connection to aesthetic gesture and religious ineffability. The neglect of silence's connection with ethics is particularly curious considering that silence is, as Ettore Rocca (2000, 77) writes, "the other aspect of the problem of communication, which has been discussed extensively." Even more, silence is mentioned in nearly all of Kierkegaard's works and is a major theme in his journals, *Fear and Trembling*, and *For Self-Examination*.

In contrast to these earlier investigations, this book provides evidence from Kierkegaard's later works, drawing mostly from *Upbuilding Discourses in Various Spirits*, *Works of Love*, and his unpublished lectures on communication to show that Kierkegaard was not only interested in what cannot be said, but also *what can be said but should not be said*. Specifically, he writes that although one can brag about one's strengths and expose others' weaknesses, one should not because they contradict the Christian imperatives to love the neighbor and imitate Christ. Silence conforms to these imperatives when it curtails excessive self-love and promotes equality through minimizing comparison with others and chatter about others' faults.

Chapter 1 introduces the central question it attempts to answer: What is the positive ethical value of silence? Two preliminary ideas are necessarily prior to this book's argument about ethical silence, and these ideas are discussed in chapters 2 and 3. First, there is a significant distinction between the first ethics (an ideal ethics consistent with Kantian ethics) and the second ethics (Kierkegaard's Christian ethics which begins with an assumption of original sin). Silence does not properly have a place within the first ethics, but is essential to the second ethics. This distinction is crucial to understanding Kierkegaard's ethics, and his writings in general, because it emphasizes his own claim that he is a "religious author" (PV 37/SKS 16:22). I believe it is impossible to strip Kierkegaard's Lutheran commitments away and still have a reasonably defensible interpretation of Kierkegaard's ethics. Second, Kierkegaard develops a theory of communication about ethics and religion in his unpublished lectures on communication, which articulates his views on *what* can be said and *how* it can be said. This theory makes a key distinction between a "communication of knowledge" which requires direct communication (i.e. through speech) and a "communication of capability" which requires indirect communication (i.e. through action). Ethical-religious communication is a "communication of capability" according to Kierkegaard, and therefore language is not sufficient for its expression.

Chapters 4 and 5 discuss Kierkegaard's views on silence, both broadly and more specifically in relation to the ethical. The heart of the book is chapter 5 in which textual evidence shows that silence plays a critical role in carrying out the imperatives of the second ethics—to imitate Christ and love the neighbor—by affirming inwardness, setting the tone for action, and equalizing the self and neighbor.

Chapter 6 discusses two exemplars of communication, Socrates and non-human life like plants and animals whose silence may be interpreted as embodying what they teach and posing puzzles to creatively engage others. Finally, in conclusion, some consequences of ethical silence are offered about the qualities of ethical teaching, freedom, and responsibility.

Chapter One

Silence in Kierkegaard's Stages

To explain his methods in his posthumous *The Point of View For My Work as an Author: A Direct Communication, Report to History*, Kierkegaard references Ecclesiastes 3:7: "There is a time to be silent and a time to speak" (PV 24/SKS 16:11). It is hard to imagine a time of Kierkegaardian silence when looking at the massive volume of published works, journal entries, and random notes he wrote between the years of 1843 and 1855. As Nancy Jay Crumbine (1975, 161) observes, ". . . of all the peculiarities of the man, Kierkegaard's most outstanding and obvious characteristic lies in the fact that language issued from him continuously . . . Kierkegaard is . . . a man dedicated to language, to communication through language, a man who lived within, through, and on behalf of language." Yet surprisingly, silence, (in Danish, *stilhed* and *tavshed*[1]) is a frequent motif in Kierkegaard's work, and as such, it can be used as a conceptual starting point to understand several aspects of Kierkegaard's philosophy. Specifically, it helps us to understand his distinction between two kinds of ethics, his critique of the limitations and misuses of language, his unique angle on religious and ethical pedagogy, and his proto-existentialism that emphasizes freedom and action. Most simply stated, Kierkegaard believed that if we could be more silent, we would be more ethical.

Before turning to all of these issues in the following chapters, it is worthwhile to consider the broad purposes of Kierkegaard's authorship. Paul Holmer (2012, 194) summarizes it succinctly: "The large story told by Kierkegaard's literature concerns the development of the human being." This is not a story to be passively received, but is rather intended to be a story in which the reader is invited to reflect and advance in their own development through reading. Kierkegaard tells part of the story by creating characters in whom readers can identify elements of themselves and who represent life views along a spectrum of development. He called this placing "*I*'s into the middle of life" (JP 1:280/Pap. VIII-2 B 82). The spectrum of development is commonly known as the stages or spheres of existence, and according to the simplest version, there are three: aesthetic, ethical, and religious. One interpretation maintains that individuals may exist or pass through these different stages during a lifetime and that each stage represents a new form of personal and spiritual maturity. Arne Grøn (2008, 133) writes that "the universally human refers to a task we all share: each individual is faced with the task of becoming a single individual. Kierkegaard calls this task *the ethical*." In developing a self, we are engaged in an ethical project. The religious stage extends this story when one becomes a self before God.

These stages are portrayed, or performed, by various characters in Kierkegaard's writings. For example, the aesthetic stage is represented by the narrator of Part I of *Either/Or*, the ethical stage finds its expression in the life and words of Judge Wilhelm in Part II of *Either/Or*, and the religious stage is the domain of Abraham and other "knights of faith." Many other Kierkegaardian characters live within or on the borders of these three stages. Since according to the traditional interpretation, these three stages lay out a progression or maturation of the individual, the religious stage is therefore, in some important sense, the "highest" point of human development. The religious stage is gained through faith, where faith is not merely the adoption of creeds and doctrines, but is fundamentally determinative of one's being. As Sheridan Hough (2015, 6) writes, ". . . faith . . . is not a thought, or a belief, but *a way of being in the world*." Some suggest that that it may be more helpful to think of the three stages of existence as *spheres* of existence in order to prevent the mistaken view that the aesthetic, ethical, or religious points of view are seen as temporary by the people within them. Rather, they are encompassing and complete forms of life,[2] and when they are traversed, they are retained and also transformed in the next sphere—for example, the aesthetic is retained and gains a new meaning in the ethical.

The concept of silence is a useful tool to distinguish these spheres; conversely, the spheres also reveal different kinds of silence. Silence does not mean one consistent thing for Kierkegaard, and he puts the concept to a variety of purposes.[3] One way to investigate these differences is to distinguish between aesthetic, ethical, and religious silence.

SILENCE IN THE 3 STAGES

Much of the previous scholarship concerning Kierkegaard's views on silence has started in context of Kierkegaard's stages of existence. Mark Taylor, for example, provides the fullest account of the varieties of silence within the basic three stages model. In "The Sounds of Silence," an essay about silence in *Fear and Trembling*, he writes that the "meaning and significance of silence are not fixed, but change from stage to stage" (Taylor 1981, 167). He describes the progression through the stages as the progression from aesthetic silence, to ethical non-silence, and finally to religious silence. Although the aesthetic and religious stages are "worlds apart" (Taylor 1981, 182), their inclusion of silence sharply differentiates them from the ethical stage.

Taylor first considers silence within the aesthetic stage. He writes that the aesthetic stage "is composed of two poles: immediacy and reflection" (Taylor 1981, 167). The first pole, immediacy, is pre-reflective and is embodied, for Kierkegaard, in the character of Don Juan from Mozart's opera. The immediate aesthetic stage is identified by an incessant striving toward sensory gratification that can only be expressed musically, because "Don Juan neither thinks nor speaks" (Taylor 1981, 168). Music, through its tonal temporality, gives expression to "motion, and hence can capture the breathless pace of Don Juan's abrupt movement from one sensual encounter to another" (Taylor 1981, 168). The spell of immediacy, in which the sensuous-erotic genius lives, would be broken by language. Don Juan cannot speak, for as soon as he does, he places himself in the category of reflection and leaves the immediate. Therefore, the silence of the immediate aesthetic is necessary.

The second pole of the aesthetic is the reflective aesthetic. Unlike with the immediate aesthetic, the silence of the reflective aesthetic is not necessary, but is chosen. Taylor (1981, 171) writes, ". . . the acquisition of the capacity to use language opens the possibility of intentional silence or deliberative concealment. Only linguistic beings can keep secrets. The reflective-aesthetic stage of existence is characterized by various modes of purposeful silence." Taylor (1981, 172) outlines four such "modes of purposeful silence" and categorizes them "*playful, deceitful, heroic,* and *demonic* silence." Playful silence is the "intentional secrecy that lies at the heart of comedy. Mistaken identity, careful disguise, white lies, puns, and irony all generate comic situations" (Taylor 1981, 172). This kind of silence may bring Shakespearean comedies to mind, but it is also "an important part of the drama of everyday life" (Taylor 1981, 172) because it is a form of play through secrecy. Deceitful silence, the second kind of purposeful silence, is used by the seducer who "develops a careful strategy to veil his real purpose" (Taylor 1981, 172). This silence is intended to benefit the one who keeps it, and comes at the expense of the one from whom the secret is hidden. Both deceitful and playful silence aim for pleasure, but deceitful silence gives pleasure only to the silent one. The third kind, demonic silence, is self-closure (*det Indesluttede*), a willful inwardness that closes the individual off from others. Taylor describes demonic silence as a sort of infatuation with alienation and suffering which the individual is not required to endure. On the contrary, the individual always has the possibility of releasing himself from his condition by "freely speaking to another" (Taylor 1981, 175). The demonically silent individual chooses silence in order to remain in his suffering condition to which he has become attached. The fourth and final form of silence in Taylor's scheme of the reflective aesthetic stage is heroic silence. This silence is the inverse of deceitful silence in terms of benefit; whereas deceitful silence benefits the silent one, heroic silence brings suffering to the silent one in order to benefit another. Johannes de silentio presents several examples of heroic silence, including that of Agamemnon who "attempts to protect those around him from unnecessary sorrow" (Taylor 1981, 177) and yet has to suffer alone in this silence as "a trial" (Taylor 1981, 177). Heroic silence appears to approach ethical silence since it is motivated by concern for the other, yet it remains in the aesthetic sphere because it aims at an aesthetic conception of happiness. For Kierkegaard, happiness belongs to the immediate, and as such it is an aesthetic rather than ethical category. Kantian ethics would also disqualify this silence as ethical because it would violate the categorical imperative by treating people as a means to their own happiness without their assent.

While silence takes many forms in the aesthetic sphere, it takes none in the ethical sphere. Whereas the aesthete is hidden in their own immediacy or reflection, the ethicist considers it their ethical duty "to become disclosed in the universal" (FT 82/SKS 4:172). Taylor's interpretation of the inappropriateness of ethical silence depends on his belief that Kierkegaard's ethics resembles Kant's ethics, in the sense that the ethical is the universal.[4] The incompatibility between silence and the ethical arises from the fundamental difference between the particularity inherent in silence and the universality demanded by ethics. Silence cannot function within the ethical sphere precisely because it indicates a prioritization of "personal desire" (Taylor 1981, 179) above the universal good. To be fully ethical, it is not enough for an agent to deny their own desires and act upon universally endorsable motivations; they must also break silence about those motivations. Ethics does not recognize the agent's motivations as ethical unless they are revealed.

The ethicist believes all forms of silence to be deceptive and deceitful. Secrecy and concealment unravel the very moral fabric of a society. Although a silent agent might act *in accordance* with duty, it is not evident to the community at large whether he acts *from* duty. Consequently the ethicist argues that a person is duty bound to speak, to come out of concealment and to reveal publicly the grounds of his deeds. Silence is a moral transgression in which one refuses to express himself in terms of universality and clings to particularity (Taylor 1981, 180).

Therefore, according to Taylor, ethics presents a two-fold requirement: 1) to act in accordance with duty, and 2) to "reveal publicly the grounds" of one's actions to show how they are motivated by duty. Therefore, the universality of the ethical stage has two aspects: it is universal in the sense that the individual's preferences are subordinated under those of the entire community, and it is also universal in the sense that its content can be explained and justified to any other rational being. Consequently, silence's negative relation to ethics amounts to a positive relation between language and ethics. Following the Kantian model, the truly free moral agent governed by reason will derive universal moral rules that apply to self and all. Rationality links moral agents through moral law and mutual understanding; "universality allows an individual to explain any moral decision to another person with the confidence that he will understand and appreciate the basis of the choice" (Taylor 1981, 180). Moral community requires the use of language to justify actions and for others to give assent to those actions. Silence cannot be ethical, therefore, because it signifies a rejection of participation with and engagement of the moral community.

As between the aesthetic and the ethical, the ethical and religious spheres are similarly distinguished from each other in terms of disclosure and concealment. Taylor (1981, 182) describes the movement from the ethical to the religious as a departure from "the ethicist's talkativeness" to the religious sphere "where we once more are able to hear the sounds of silence." The religious sphere brings back an emphasis on the particularity of the individual, but now in relation to God. Taylor (1981, 186) writes, "the direct, unmediated, radically privatized and individualized relation of the believer to God cannot be conveyed in the universal categories of thought and language." Religious silence is not motivated by a purposeful desire to withhold, but rather is caused by the ineffable character of the relationship between God and the individual. In other words, the individual in the religious stage does not remain silent by choice, but from necessity. Taylor (1981, 185) writes, "not only is the believer unable to express himself to others; he cannot even make his trial comprehensible to himself. Faith involves an absolute paradox that shatters human reflection."

Taylor's view on the relation of silence to the three stages of existence, in its most simplified form,[5] is outlined in the table below.

AESTHETIC		ETHICAL	RELIGIOUS
immediate	reflective		
	1. playful	X	
	2. deceitful		
	3. heroic		
	4. demonic		
necessary silence	*not necessary silence*		*necessary silence*

Figure 1.1. Created by S. Hay.

Silence has a place in the aesthetic and religious stages, and depending on its form, it can be either necessary or unnecessary (i.e., one *can* break silence but purposefully does not). Silence has no place within the ethical.

SILENCE BEYOND THE 3 STAGES

The aim of the rest of this book is to add a new dimension to the view just presented. While Taylor's view has good explanatory value for Kierkegaard's earliest works, particularly *Fear and Trembling*, it is incomplete in respect to the works in Kierkegaard's second authorship. In these later works, like *Works of Love* and *Upbuilding Discourses in Various Spirits*, Kierkegaard offers his readers an idea of ethical silence, a silence that expresses love and humility, a silence that may ultimately present an even greater challenge to our contemporary status quo than to Kierkegaard's own time.

This new interpretation shows that Kierkegaard considers the purposeful use of silence within his second ethics. As Arne Grøn (2008, 133) points out, "the ethical seems to change meaning in Kierkegaard's later works. Kierkegaard indicates in *The Concept of Anxiety* that it is necessary to distinguish between meanings of the ethical . . . he distinguishes between what he calls the first and second ethics." Silence in this second ethics is not the same as the ineffable of the religious stage. It is not the silence of what *cannot* be said, but rather is the silence of what *should not* be said.

AESTHETIC		ETHICAL (1)	RELIGIOUS		ETHICAL (2)
immediate	reflective		A	B	
necessary silence	*not necessary silence*	X	*necessary silence*	*necessary silence*	*not necessary silence*

Figure 1.2. Created by S. Hay.

NOTES

1. While both *tavshed* and *stilhed* translate to silence, *tavshed* is connected to secrecy and *stilhed* also means stillness and calm.

2. See, for example, C. Stephen Evans (2004, 48) who writes, "We can therefore think of the aesthetic and ethical stances not merely as stages that one lives through, but as existential spheres which can define a person's life as a whole. They confront each other as rival views of how life should be lived, mutually exclusive existential standpoints."

3. As Edward F. Mooney (2007, 236) puts it, "Even if one were to think of 'silence' as a pervasive Kierkegaardian theme, one would have to distinguish an array of differences that are mostly likely too varied to yield to a single, all-purpose account."

4. Roland Green (1992, 95) concurs with this position in his book, *Kierkegaard and Kant: The Hidden Debt*, in which he writes that a "major and overarching area of similarity between Kierkegaard and Kant has to do with their shared conviction that 'the ethical is the universal.'"

5. Taylor also mentions that there are two forms of religiosity on p. 167, but does not make an explicit distinction between Religiousness A and Religiousness B in his discussion of silence and the religious in his article.

Chapter Two

Kierkegaard's Ethics

In the introduction to *The Concept of Anxiety: A Simple Psychologically Orienting Deliberation on the Dogmatic Issue of Hereditary Sin*, Kierkegaard's pseudonym, Vigilius Haufniensis, distinguishes between a first (psychological) ethics and a second (dogmatic) ethics. Haufniensis's explicit distinction between the two ethics is supported by an implicit distinction found throughout Kierkegaard's authorship; the first ethics is employed in *Fear and Trembling* and *Either/Or*, while the second ethics is extensively elaborated in his writings after *Concluding Unscientific Postscript*, those which belong to his "second authorship."[1] This later period contains a more comprehensive picture of Kierkegaard's views on the relationship between Christianity and how one is to live, and culminated in his sharp polemic against the Danish church. Kierkegaard's second ethics is developed in *Practice in Christianity* (1850), *Upbuilding Discourses in Various Spirits* (1847), *Christian Discourses* (1848), and most notably in *Works of Love* (1847).

Simply stated, the first ethics is a rationally derived and ideal ethics, one that broadly matches the ethical as described in Kant's *Groundwork of the Metaphysic of Morals* and Hegel's *Elements of the Philosophy of Right*. Although Hegel's system of ethics differs from that of Kant, both systems form the theoretical background against which Kierkegaard develops the second ethics as a radical alternative. The differences between the first and second ethics are numerous, but their divergence is best seen through the opposing ways they account for the origin and justification of ethics.

THE FIRST ETHICS

Haufniensis labels the first ethics as an "ideal science" that "proposes to bring ideality into actuality" (CA 16/SKS 4:324). It begins with ideality, and as a science, it finds its justification in reason.

The first ethics begins with ideality, or the realm of the ethical ideal as a mental abstraction of ethical perfection. The attempt to conceptualize moral perfection can be traced back to classical Greece. For example, in *Nicomachean Ethics*, Aristotle's (1987, 386) conception of virtue, or moral excellence, is described as *sophrosyne*, "a mean . . . between two vices, the one involving excess, the other deficiency." According to this view, ethical perfection is the attainment of the "intermediate in passions and in actions" (Aristotle 1987, 386). The "intermediate" is determined by the mind; it is "determined by reason and in the way in which the man of practical wisdom would determine it" (Aristotle 1987, 383). One has to have a great deal of self-knowledge and knowledge about the conditions of the world in order to strike this perfect ethical balance.

Ethical systems during the Enlightenment also attempted to define ethical ideality. In the preface to *Groundwork of the Metaphysic of Morals*, Kant (1964, 60) explained his goal "to seek out and establish the supreme principle of morality." This supreme principle, the categorical imperative, is the moral law that each rational being derives and bestows upon themself. The categorical imperative is violated when we are governed by inclination or motivations other than rationally determined duty. Other examples of ethical ideality include Hegel's *Sittlichkeit*, Judge William's concept of marital duty in *Either/Or*, and Johannes de silentio's interpretation in *Fear and Trembling* of the political good of Agamemnon's sacrifice of Iphigenia. The common element in all of these examples is that they are all products of the ethicist's reflections on the nature of ethical perfection.

Ethical ideality begins as a concept, but then seeks its actualization in the world. The balancing act required by Aristotle's version of moral excellence is not merely something to be pondered in the realm of ideas, but is something that is to be put in practice and habituated. He writes, ". . . we are inquiring not in order to know what excellence is, but in order to become good, since otherwise our inquiry would have been no use" (Aristotle 1987, 377). Likewise, Kant (1964, 58) intended his version of the ethical ideal to find its place in actuality, or "the field of action." In one of the greatest titled essays of all time, "On the Old Saw: That May be Right in Theory But It Won't Work in Practice," Kant argues that the purpose of theory is its implementation, otherwise theory is worthless. Within the first ethics, ethical activity, as described by Haufniensis, is a *downward* movement from ideality to actuality. He writes, "Ethics proposes to bring ideality into actuality. On the other hand, it is not the nature of its movement to raise actuality up into ideality" (CA 16/SKS 4:324). Both Aristotle's and Kant's ethics follow this pattern of movement; perfection is established through the exercise of reason, as we, as ethical agents, are to bring the idea down into the world.

Because ethical ideality is a mental construct (as a concept) and it places demands on actuality (as moral law or moral excellence), it has a particular two-fold nature: the ethical ideal is the first ethics' starting point (what the individual must *attempt* to become ethical), and at the same time is the first ethics' ending point (what the individual must *achieve* to become ethical). Ethical ideality is therefore descriptive and prescriptive; it can describe the moral law and requires the execution of moral law. In its prescriptive role, ethical ideality applies itself to actuality through the demand of moral law. Reason not only generates the ethical ideal, it also justifies it.

Reason's joint role as imperative maker and imperative justifier is particularly clear in Kant's work. He writes, "Everyone must admit that a law has to carry with it absolute necessity if it is to be valid morally—valid, that is, as a ground of obligation . . . consequently the ground of obligation must be looked for, not in the nature of man nor in the circumstances of the world in which he is placed, but solely *a priori* in the concepts of pure reason" (Kant 1964, 57). Reason validates moral law, serves as a "ground of obligation," and thereby makes it necessary. The necessity produced by reason is contrasted with the contingent and unstable conditions created by particular circumstance, unique personality, and fleeting inclinations. Moral law is not, for Kant, something particular to each situation or person, but is fixed and permanent; reason as the foundation of necessity is precisely what creates its permanence and stability. Therefore, the categorical imperative, the statement of ethical ideality, and a product of pure reason, is moral law.

The necessity of moral law leads to the necessity of moral action when reason and the will are harmonized. Kant (1964, 80) writes, "If reason infallibly determines the will, then in a being of this kind the actions which are recognized to be objectively necessary are also subjectively necessary—that is to say, the will is then a power to choose only that which reason independently of inclination recognizes to be practically necessary, that is, to be good." But, as Kant (1954, 80) notes, "as actually happens in the case of men" the will and reason are not always perfectly attuned to each other. When reason and will do not correspond, "then actions which are recognized to be objectively necessary are subjectively contingent" (Kant 1964, 80), and this gives rise to the possibility of moral error. Because the will does not naturally and spontaneously choose good actions all the time, it falls to reason to *necessitate* the good. Reason is able to do this by commanding the will through the imperative, which is, in Kant's (1964, 81) words, "the formula of this command."

Reason not only necessitates moral law, it also makes moral law universal. It is universal in the sense that anyone who is rational can derive the moral law, as well as in the sense that the moral law applies to everyone. Kant (1964, 79) maintains that the ethical ideal is not just produced by the expert philosopher, but rather it springs from "the most ordinary human reason just as much as in the most highly speculative." Furthermore, he states that, "human reason can, in matters of morality, be easily brought to a high degree of accuracy and precision even in the most ordinary intelligence" (Kant 1964, 59). Anybody with reason can conceptualize the content of moral perfection, and therefore everybody with reason possesses access to the moral law.

The universality of moral law in the second sense means its demands for action are the same for everyone. Kant's (1964, 70) categorical imperative has this aspect of universalization built directly into it: its first formulation states, "I ought never act except in such a way *that I can also will that my maxim should become a universal law*." Moral law is universally derivable, and also universally applicable. Exceptions for the particularity of individuals violate this law because, according to this system, our shared rationality equates the interests of the individual with the interests of the whole. Kierkegaard portrays this sense of morality's universalization through the character of Judge William in *Either/Or*. According to Judge William: "The person who views life ethically sees the universal, and the person who lives ethically expresses the universal in his life. He makes himself the universal human being, not by taking off his concretion, for then he becomes a complete nonentity, but by putting it on and interpenetrating it with the universal" (EO 2:256/SKS 3:243).

The appeal of reason's role for ethics is significant, because reason's necessity and universality rule out other philosophically unacceptable alternatives, namely relativism and dogmatism. Relativism is avoided because reason ensures that ethics has stability and "will not split up . . . into a multiplicity of particular stipulations" (EO 2:254/SKS 3:242). And dogmatism is avoided because reason ensures that everyone can determine and apply the principles of morality for oneself, rather than having to accept ethical principles given from and judged by an external authority. Kant's essay "What is Enlightenment?" presents a compelling case for the political maturation of individuals through their own exercise of rational judgment rather than taking someone else's word for it.[2] Hegel also believed that ethical truth must be comprehended by reason, and not merely accepted from the government, popular opinion, or by one's gut feelings.

> The *truth* concerning *right, ethics, and the state* is at any rate *as old* as its *exposition and promulgation* in *public laws and in public morality and religion*. What more does this truth require, inasmuch as the thinking mind is not content to possess it in this proximate manner? What it needs is to be *comprehended* as well, so that the context which is already rational in itself may also

gain a rational form and thereby appear justified to free thinking. For such thinking does not stop at what is *given*, whether the latter is supported by the external positive authority of the state or of mutual agreement among human beings, or by the authority of inner feelings and the heart and by the testimony of the spirit which immediately concurs with this, but starts out from itself and thereby demands to know itself as united in its innermost being with the truth. (Hegel 1991, 11)

Reason's ultimate superiority and authority is clear in Kant's and Hegel's ethical systems. Reason not only establishes what has ethical value (namely, through the categorical imperative and other expressions of the ethical ideal), and validates what has ethical value (through its properties of necessity and universality), but it also has value in itself. Reason, in the first ethics, may be interpreted as morality's "first principle," without which morality gives way to the chaos of relativism or to the fatalism of dogmatism. Hegel quotes Mephistopheles in a passage of *Faust* in the preface to *Elements of the Philosophy of Right* that reveals the danger inherent in reason's absence:

> Reason and knowledge mayst thou well despise,
> the highest strength in man that lie—
> and even if my charge he weren't, there's naught could save him-
> he'll be destroyed for evermore![3] (Goethe 1963, 146)

These words are a warning, acutely felt by Hegel, that to lose hold on reason is equivalent to handing oneself over to the devil. Hegel writes of "superficial philosophy" (Hegel 1991, 15) that bases science on "immediate perception and contingent imagination" and "reduce[s] the complex inner articulation of the ethical . . . to a must of heart, friendship, and enthusiasm" (Hegel 1991, 15–16). Without the careful use of reason, ethical philosophy has no substance, stability, nor legitimacy.

Although the first ethics is primarily a "philosophical ethics"[4] derived from human reason, its proponents (Kant, Hegel, Judge William) consider it to be not only consistent with Christian religious belief, but also requiring it. However, as Anthony Rudd correctly points out, their version of Christianity is not the same as Kierkegaard's version which makes "greater demands;"

> . . . Kierkegaard did not have much to say specifically in criticism of an atheistic, secular approach to ethics. Rather, he starts from the existing religious consciousness within the ethics, which typically assumes that we relate to God mainly by the simple performance of our social duties. . . . Kierkegaard aims to show those at the ethical level that religion makes greater demands than they have been willing to acknowledge. This presents them with a dilemma: they must either stay at the level of social morality, and accept that they are not religious in any decisive sense, or they must move to a more seriously religious level. (Rudd 1993, 116)

THE SECOND ETHICS

While the first ethics originates in ideality and is justified by reason, the second ethics originates in actuality and is justified by faith.

Although the first and second ethics are distinct, they are not unrelated; the second ethics begins at the point where the first ethics eventually fails. The second ethics interprets the first ethics' failure to occur at the point where ethical ideality is supposed to be lived out in actuality. This difficulty is expressed by Aristotle (1987, 385) who states that "it is no easy task to be good." For the second ethics, this may be understatement; in fact, it is impossible for humans to reach the ideal's goal of ethical perfection. Vigilius Haufniensis writes that the first ethics "points to ideality as a task and assumes that every man possesses the requisite conditions" (CA 16/SKS 4:324). This is consistent with Kantian ethics which maintains that the rational being as both moral legislator and moral subject can carry out the imperatives oneself imposes, therefore bridging the intelligible and sensible worlds: "The moral 'I ought' is thus an "I will' for man as a member of the intelligible world; and it is conceived by him as an 'I ought' only in so far as he considers himself at the same time to be a member of the sensible world" (Kant 1964, 123). However, the assumption that "every man possesses the requisite conditions" is, from the second ethics' perspective, an incorrect assumption.

Human freedom poses the obvious problem for the first ethics; we are able to do the ethical action *and* able to do the unethical action. Plato argues that ignorance is the reason why we knowingly do wrong. For Aristotle and Kant, it is due to desire or inclination overruling reason. For Kant (1964, 114), "a free will and a will under moral laws are one and the same" precisely because for him freedom is defined as being governed by reason, as opposed to being captive to variable inclinations. No matter what explanations are provided for weakness of will,[5] its mere existence presents a challenge to ethics based on ideality. This challenge comes from the mismatch between the ideality of moral imperatives and the actuality of human action.[6] Haufniensis characterizes the first ethics as producing and exacerbating this mismatch:

> The more ideal ethics is, the better. It must not permit itself to be distracted by the babble that it is useless to require the impossible. For even to listen to such talk is unethical and is something for which ethics has neither *time* nor *opportunity*. (CA 17/SKS 4:324)

By requiring the impossible, the first ethics cannot find its way to "the field of action" (Kant 1964, 58), and it "develops a contradiction" (CA 16/SKS 4:324) by demanding something be done that cannot be done. The resulting dead-end of the first ethics is where it is "shipwrecked" (CA 17/SKS 4:324), creating a point of departure for the second ethics.

The second ethics begins with a consciousness of the impossibility of meeting the ethical ideal, a consciousness of the actual human situation of moral fallibility.[7] This starting point is where the moral agent *is*, rather than where the moral agent *wants* to be. The second ethics does not follow the pattern of movement of the first ethics which is downward from ideality to actuality, but instead establishes a human-based pattern of movement, upward from actuality to ideality.

Within the second ethics, actuality, or the morally imperfect nature of humans, is transposed through theological terminology as sinfulness, also described as hereditary sin, a universal human condition.[8] This means it is not simply that people make mistakes in moral matters that prevent them from reaching ideality's demands, but rather that people are unavoidably morally deficient. The moral challenge is not that we lack understanding about what to do, but that we fail to do it. This idea of unavoidable sinfulness is the pivotal concept between the first and second ethics.

> The first ethics was shipwrecked on the sinfulness of the single individual. Therefore, instead of being able to explain this sinfulness, the first ethics fell into an even greater and ethically more enigmatic difficulty, since the sin of the individual expanded into the sin of the whole race. At this point, dogmatics came to the rescue with hereditary sin. The new ethics presupposes dogmatics, and by means of hereditary sin it explains the sin of the single individual, while at the same time it sets ideality as a task, not from a movement from above and downward but from below and upward. (CA 20/SKS 4:329)

The significance of hereditary sin cannot be overemphasized, for here we see the change from psychological (conceptual) ethics to dogmatic (religious) ethics. Hereditary sin explains ethical ideality's nonexistence in the world, and it also introduces the dogmatic vocabulary of faith.

As discussed in the preceding section, reason produces and justifies the ethical idea in the first ethics. The second ethics looks instead to faith as the basis for its definition and justification. Haufniensis writes that "the new ethics presupposes dogmatics" (CA 20/SKS 4:329). This presupposition is no small matter, for it radically changes the way that ethics is to be thought about and enacted.

Kierkegaard firmly holds that speculative reason goes beyond its proper limit when it enters the realms of religion and ethics.[9] Committing oneself to be religious or atheistic, ethical or unethical, involves a decision that is prior to accepting or rejecting arguments or reasons. To be religious or ethical is a kind of life stance in which reasons and arguments cannot take hold unless there is a predisposition to that point of view already within the individual.

Alastair MacIntyre (1984, 40) describes this when he imagines someone who is undecided on the issue of ethics:

> Suppose that someone confronts the choice between them having as yet embraced neither [the ethical nor the aesthetic]. He can be offered no *reason* for preferring one to the other. For if a given reason offers support for the ethical way of life—to live in that way will serve the demands of duty *or* to live in that way will be to accept moral perfection as a goal and so give a certain kind of meaning to one's actions—the person who has not yet embraced either the ethical or the aesthetic still has to choose whether or not to treat this reason as having any force. If it already has force for him, he has already chosen the ethical; which *ex hypothesi* he has not. And so it is also with reasons supportive to the aesthetic. The man who has not yet chosen has still to choose whether to treat them as having force. He still has to choose his first principles, and just because they are *first* principles, prior to any others in the chain of reasoning, no more ultimate reasons can be adduced to support them.

The "force" of a reason, or argument, depends on some prior decision made within the individual, a decision that makes the individual willing or unwilling to finally accept the reason or argument. Kierkegaard's emphasis falls on the importance of choice, rather than reasons,[10] in the appropriation of a religious or ethical form of life. His ethics shifts away from determining the content and justification of ethics toward a lived commitment to its content. Therefore, persuasion to become religious or ethical is not the task of the persuader, but rather the task of the persuaded; the burden falls on the one that is undecided, not on the efficacy of the one trying to convince. Kierkegaard writes,

> There is no direct communication and no direct reception: there is a choice. It does not take place, as in direct communication, with coaxing and threatening and admonishing—and then, then, quite imperceptibly, little by little comes the transition, the transition to accepting it more or less, to keeping oneself convinced of it, to being of the opinion etc. No, a very specific kind of reception is required—that of faith. And faith itself is a dialectical qualification. Faith is a choice, certainly not direct reception—and the recipient is the one who is disclosed, whether he will believe or be offended. (PC 140–41/SKS 12:145)

Choice in ultimately relevant matters, like religion and ethics, is a matter of faith for Kierkegaard, precisely because it is made without recourse to reasons. The charge of irrationality aimed at Kierkegaard shows a misunderstanding of Kierkegaard's view about how and when reasons work; it is not that Kierkegaard is hostile to reason, but instead he is adamant about the error of reason's over-extension in domains where it does not have the role we assume. The objectivity and disinterestedness required by reason result in an incorrect, even contradictory, vantage point from which to think about and engage in religion and ethics whose subject is existence. Not only does Kierkegaard believe that reason is inapplicable to ethics and religion, but he also calls into question the very possibility of "pure" reason.[11] He writes,

> Human reason has boundaries; that is where the negative concepts are to be found. Boundary disputes are negative, constraining. But people have a rattle-brained, conceited notion about human reason, especially in our age, when one never thinks of a thinker, a reasonable person, but thinks of pure reason and the like, which simply does not exist, since no one, be he professor or what he will, is pure reason. Pure reason is something fantastical, and the limitless fantastical belongs where there are no negative concepts, and one understands everything like the sorcerer who ended by eating his own stomach. (JP 1:7/ SKS 23:21)

However, in the absence of reason's justification, a problem arises for ethics. The problem centers on ethical authority and has two aspects: 1) without reason, there is no insurance that the ethical agent will make the *correct* choice, and 2) without reason, ethics no longer binds the agent to ethical action in the same sense (i.e., in the way that reason had necessitated it). These two aspects of the problem roughly match the concerns for justification for the definition of and obligation to the moral imperative. Within the second ethics, the stress has been placed on the activity of choice, not on which particular choice to make or how to bind obligation to the choice. MacIntyre (1984, 42) poses the problem this way: ". . . the ethical is to have authority over us. But how can that which we adopt for no reason have any authority over us?"

This problem points precisely to the heart of the contrast between the first and second ethics. The first ethics relies on reason to derive the moral imperative; the second ethics holds that God, more specifically the God of Christianity, dictates the moral imperative. The first ethics compels the agent to moral action through the necessity and universality of reason; the second ethics maintains that the individual's obligation to moral law is based on a commitment they make. Therefore, in the second ethics, both aspects of moral justification (for the definition of the imperative and the obligation for moral behavior) as based in religious faith. This faith entails as belief in a God that makes moral demands and a belief that God's demands should be fulfilled. For Kierkegaard, the authority of the second ethics is the authority of Christianity.

It is interesting to note that the second ethics returns ethics to a position from which Kierkegaard's predecessors during the Enlightenment were trying to pull away, namely ethics as a dogmatic given. In this way, Kierkegaard may be seen as contributing "a new practical and philosophical underpinning for an older and inherited way of life" (MacIntyre 1984, 43). Kierkegaard does not offer a new system of ethics, but rather an interpretation of how the free individual chooses this way of life. As opposed to his philosophical predecessors, Kierkegaard does not envision the pinnacle of human accomplishment to be the exercise of rationality, but rather the passionate movement of faith.

Because the second ethics places emphasis on the choice and action of the ethical agent rather than on their rational capacities, Kierkegaard was suspicious of the kind of extended ethical reflection required by the first ethics. In "Ethical Reflection as Evasion," Compaijen and Vos (2019, 67) write that for Kierkegaard, "ethical reflection can be—and, as a matter of fact, frequently *is*—a clever way of evading ethical action and life." They argue that there are two ways to understand this evasion: 1) "ethical reflection can be . . . a process in which the reflective agent radically detaches herself from (what we would call) her 'existential situation'" (Compaijen and Vos 2019, 68) and, 2) ethical reflection "can be an evasion when it is directed toward acquiring knowledge that will enable the agent to answer the questions of what one should do or how one should live" (Compaijen and Vos 2019, 68). The second ethics does not endorse the "disengaged standpoint" (Compaijen and Vos 2019, 68) or the acquisition of knowledge because the ethical requires engaged subjectivity and the "transition from knowledge to realization" (Compaijen and Vos 2019, 69). For the second ethics, the ethical agent must shift from detachment to attachment, from asking about what should be done to doing what should be done.

THE IMPERATIVES OF THE SECOND ETHICS

There are two main imperatives in the second ethics which dictate what should be done by moral agents. The first imperative, the command to love the neighbor, is addressed primarily in *Works of Love*. The second imperative, the command to imitate Christ, is addressed primarily in *Practice in Christianity*. Both imperatives are scripturally based, rather than conceptually or rationally based, are therefore divine commands. The acceptance of these imperatives as true and binding is subjective, and as such is a matter of faith. The great presupposition of the second ethics is the presupposition of dogmatics; in other words, that moral law is given by God and is accepted through faith.

In the "First Series" of *Works of Love*, Kierkegaard centers his "Christian deliberations" (WL 3/SKS 9:11) around two scriptural texts: Matthew 22:29 ("But the second commandment is like it: You shall love your neighbor as yourself") and Romans 13:10 ("Love does no wrong to a neighbor; therefore love is the fulfilling of the law"). In the Matthew text, Jesus is asked which of the commandments is greatest, and he replies, "On these two commandments [to love God and to love the neighbor] depend all the law and the prophets."

He sets a new moral agenda, one that recognizes the authority of Judaic law, but has its own ethical priorities. Within Christianity, the imperative to love the neighbor is the moral law given through the revelation of Jesus.

The meaning of this imperative depends on the specific meanings of *love* and *the neighbor*. The meanings of these words are connected because they both resist preference, either self-love or love for a particular person. Preferential love, including erotic love and friendship, are described as forms of self-love by Kierkegaard.

> In erotic love and friendship, the two love each other by virtue of the dissimilarity or by virtue of the similarity that is based on dissimilarity (as when two friends love each other by virtue of similar customs, characters, occupations, education, etc., that is, on the basis of the similarity by which they are different from other people, or in which there are like each other as different from other people). Therefore the two can become one self in a selfish sense. (WL 56/SKS 9:61)

On the other hand, Christian love, or *agape*, is love based in self-denial. The self-denial of Christianity does two things: 1) it acknowledges that we usually look out for ourselves first and can get carried away with our interests, and 2) it deliberately thwarts that tendency so that we make room to consider others. Sometimes self-denial can be misunderstood outside the Christian context as self-hatred, or simply a lack of care for oneself. These distortions of self-denial show why a humanistic ethics does not show deep enough self-knowledge for Kierkegaard. *Agape* is not love that arises naturally in people, and therefore it needs to be imposed in the form of a commandment: "Erotic love and friendship are preferential love and the passion of preferential love; Christian love is self-denial's love, for which this *shall* vouches" (WL 52/SKS 9:59). Christian love purposefully removes preference from the act of loving so that love is liberated from the changeable tastes of the lover and the contingent qualities of the beloved. It does not depend on the wishes of the lover (i.e., to love a certain type of person instead of another type, or to love a particular person instead of another one), nor does it depend on the attributes possessed by the beloved (i.e., their measure of lovableness or their admirable qualities). Christian love allows for no distinctions to be made among people as objects of love: "The Christian doctrine, on the contrary, is to love the neighbor, to love the whole human race, all people, even the enemy, and not to make exceptions, neither of preference nor of aversion" (WL 19/SKS 9:27).

Christian love has as its object "the whole human race, all people." As a result, it is inextricably linked to the Christian concept of neighbor: "If it were not a duty to love, the concept 'neighbor' would not exist either; but only when one loves the neighbor, only then is the selfishness in preferential love rooted out and the equality of the eternal preserved" (WL 44/SKS 9:51).

Since "the neighbor is all people" (WL 55/SKS 9:62), the concept of the neighbor is what ensures the universal application of Christian love which shows no partiality. The neighbor remains unspecified, and remains open to include every particular person. The neighbor as the universal object of the requirement to love lies at the center of the first imperative.

Although the object of Christian love is universalized, the subject of Christian love is not. Unlike the first ethics in which the imperative is placed on the universal subject ("moral laws have to hold for every rational being as such" [Kant 1964, 79]), the second ethics requires love from the single faithful individual. In Kierkegaard's view, the second ethics' demand can come in direct conflict with the secular ethical demands of the first ethics. When such a conflict arises, such as in the case of Abraham in *Fear and Trembling*, it is a test of faith for the ethical agent.

The frequent complaint of Kierkegaard's focus on the individual at the expense of the community misses Kierkegaard's point. Those who criticize Kierkegaard for holding, in their view, an anti-social position that has little relevance in our post-Marxist world where much hinges on sociality, politics, and human relationship, fail to grasp why Kierkegaard thought the focus on the individual was important.[12] It is important because it constitutes a primary identity that provides the foundation for genuine relationship. It is precisely in his second ethics that he opens a true space for connection between people; the individual is to first develop in order to relate to others. He writes, "Not until the single individual has established an ethical stance despite the whole world, not until then can there be any question of genuinely uniting; otherwise it gets to be a union of people who separately are weak, a union as unbeautiful and depraved as a child marriage" (TA 106/SKS 8:101). *Works of Love*, Kierkegaard's strongest refutation to the charge of exclusive focus on the individual, moreover presents a radical view of love that challenges convention and political order because it "promotes the equality of the eternal" (Pérez-Álvarez 2009, 70).

In *Works of Love*, Kierkegaard writes, "Love is the fulfilling of the Law" (WL 106/SKS 9:110), and also writes that "Christ was the fulfilling of the Law" (WL 101/SKS 9:106). Therefore, Jesus is to be understood as the embodiment of Christian love: "he [Jesus] was Love, and his love was the fulfilling of the Law" (WL 99/SKS 9:103). Jesus was "one with every single requirement of the Law" (WL 99/SKS 9:104), and so his life is the exemplification of perfected Christian ethics. The command to imitate Christ is the second imperative of the second ethics.

Imitation of Christ is differentiated from both being Christ and admiring Christ. Being Christ is an impossibility, not only from a practical standpoint (either Jesus was a historical figure who has long since died, or he is a character of a fictitious scriptural narrative who has never lived), but also from a theological standpoint (to claim to be Christ is blasphemy[13] to Christianity). Whereas being Christ requires too much, admiring Christ requires too little. The stance of the admirer is that of an observer at a safe distance rather than that of an active participant. The imitation of Christ, in contrast, involves the active shaping of one's life to the pattern of Christ's life. That one's life could never be exactly like Christ's is not the relevant point because "to be an imitator means that life has as much similarity to his [Jesus'] as is possible for a human life to have" (PC 106/SKS 12:114).

The first and second imperatives are closely linked; the first imperative is a call to love in the broadest sense and the second imperative is a call to love following the perfect, concrete example of love. It is impossible to say which imperative is more important or more strenuous. In one regard, the first imperative to love the neighbor appears more difficult because its demand cannot be fulfilled with any set of specific actions, and in fact, extends beyond the specific set of Jesus' actions. On this point, Saez Tajafuerce (1998, 75fn) writes that she would not be "unconditionally willing to read the notion of love of the neighbor in the light of concrete actions such as Christ's actions in the world as we know them from the Gospel." She notes that a tension arises between a literal interpretation of imitation and a notion of love "which is not and does not want to be determined by immediacy" (Saez Tajafuerce 1998, 75). She points to Kierkegaard's passage in *Works of Love* that states, "There is no work, not one single one, not even the best, about which we unconditionally dare to say: The one who does this unconditionally demonstrates love by it" (WL 13/SKS 9:21). Saez Tajafuerce (1998, 67fn) maintains, I think correctly, that "Christian love, as Kierkegaard presents it in *WOL*, is and remains the new qualification of immediacy and never . . . the other way around."

Yet, in another regard, the second imperative to imitate Christ appears to be more difficult, since within Christian theology Christ is understood as the incarnation of God and humans are necessarily infinitely far from being God. The ideality established by these two imperatives, therefore, becomes practically unreachable, and once again, as in the case of the first ethics, a gulf opens between what ethics demands and human ability. The gulf is particularly revealed in Kierkegaard's comments about his own ability to be Christian; "Never have I . . . said: I am the true Christian . . . No . . . *I know what Christianity is*; I myself acknowledge my defects as a Christian" (PV 15/SKS 13:23).

However, just as Christian dogmatics provided an explanation for the failure of the first ethics by introducing the concept of hereditary sin, Christian dogmatics also provides a solution to the gulf between the imperatives of the second ethics and human ability. Christian dogmatics bridges this gulf through two concepts: striving and grace. Kierkegaard writes, "*Christianly* the emphasis does not fall so much upon to what extent or how far a person succeeds in meeting or fulfilling the requirement, if he is actually striving, as upon his getting an impression of the requirement in all its infinitude so that he rightly learns to be humbled and to rely on grace" (JP 1:993/SKS 24:163).

The ethical agent is to strive towards ethics' ideality by attempting to fulfill its demands to the best of their ability. At the point at which the agent can go no further, the gulf is filled by God through grace. Yet grace is not to be regarded as a mechanism which lightens the moral load, weakens the magnitude of the imperatives, nor excuses the agent from vigorous striving. Rather, grace is to be regarded as the means by which actuality is to reach to ideality; it allows for the completion of ethics, for ethics to work "out all right" (PV 16/SKS 13:25) in the end.

Although the concepts of striving and grace close the gulf that "shipwrecked" the first ethics, the attempt to actualize the second ethics poses another problem. This other problem arises from the ambiguous and necessarily open nature of the concepts employed in the two ethical imperatives. Although the ethical agent is meant to strive, they are not given specific instruction on how to meet the imperatives demands. Saez Tajafuerce (1998, 69) discusses Adorno's formulation[14] of this problem in the case of the first imperative to love the neighbor:

> The point now, according to Adorno is that, to consider the category of the neighbor in such abstract terms dismisses and eliminates all 'particular reality' and, in so doing, the very realm of action as well as action itself are disregarded. In his denial of 'reification,' a denial of which Adorno approves, Kierkegaard unfortunately makes the neighbor disappear: 'the Christian neighbor loses the concreteness which alone made it possible to behave concretely towards him' and consequently, he makes love disappear.

The same problem of ambiguity applies to the second imperative. Exactly how far is the ethical agent able to imitate Christ? Exactly how much imitation is sufficient? Exactly how much similarity to Jesus' life "is possible for a human life to have" (PC 106/SKS 12:114)?

Saez Tajafeurce argues persuasively for a solution to this perceived problem of abstraction. She writes that the concepts contained within the imperatives[15] are intentionally abstract, and as such, resist attempts at complete description. "The working Christian love, therefore, does not care about taking a 'concrete' shape, because no 'concrete' shape embodies it to its full and exhaustive expression" (Saez Tajafeurce 1998, 69fn). Christian love, the neighbor, and the various ways to imitate Christ are impossible to capture in their entirety. Kierkegaard writes in the preface to *Works of Love* that although he takes "works of love" to be the subject of his deliberations, he does not claim to have enumerated all of their possible manifestations, or to have completely described one of their instances:

> [These deliberations] are about *works of love*, not as if hereby all its works were now added up and described, oh, far from it; not as if even the particular work described were described once and for all. . . . Something that in its total richness is *essentially* inexhaustible is also in its smallest work *essentially* indescribable just because essentially it is totally present everywhere and *essentially* cannot be described. (WL 3/SKS 9:11)

If works of love are "*essentially* inexhaustible" and "*essentially* indescribable," then it seems that discussion of an ethics that is based on the duty to love must find its end here, for no account of this ethics can be a complete and final systematization. Although one quickly reaches the end of the second ethics' description, this end is meant to mark the beginning of the second ethics' activity. The true work of the second ethics does not consist in deriving ethical principles nor in insuring their legitimacy. Rather, the second ethics wants its agents to get on with it. The second ethics presupposes the legitimacy of its imperatives through an act of faith and begins its work in the realm of actuality where humans are recognized to be morally imperfect, but yet are to strive towards an ultimate ethical ideality. Both of the imperatives of the second ethics demand that something should be *done*, namely *to love* and *to imitate* Christ, and thereby incite the moral agent to action. In the second ethics, focus is placed on action, instead of reflection or conceptualization. Saez Tajafuerce (1998, 73) writes, "the second ethics is not about knowing one's duties, but about fulfilling a duty."

It is valuable to view both of the second ethics' imperatives as action-based. Saez Tajafuerce (1998, 66) offers a possible reading that translates the concept of 'the neighbor' directly into 'a task':

> . . . a radically pragmatic reading of the neighbor from the perspective of Christian love does not allow a substantive understanding of it. . . . The fulfilling of the Law, the accomplishment of the task and, so, the configuration of every work of love leaves behind a trace; it draws a very specific movement where the neighbor is to be found . . . Linked to God, the neighbor could not possible be considered as an 'object of admiration' but only of Christian love and, as such, an object of action. And to be an object of action is nothing but to be a *task*.

This reading denies purely abstract content to 'the neighbor' and centers understanding the neighbor on the activity of Christian love as love's task. The second imperative to imitate Christ should also be read as a task. Christ is like the neighbor in this regard, who "could not possibly be considered as an 'object of admiration'" but is rather an object of activity. The task is to emulate, not to applaud from a distance; "he is indeed a *requirement* upon me to give him back in replica" (PC 243/SKS 12:237). An understanding of the two imperatives stops the activity of ethical reflection and thrusts the moral agent immediately into action. The end of ethical reflection marks the end of language, giving away to action and silence.

NOTES

1. Bruce Kirmmse (1990, 263) writes in *Kierkegaard in Golden Age Denmark* that,

> The seven major pseudonymous works from February 1843 to February 1846 . . . have generally attracted most of the attention which scholars have given to SK, and from a philosophical and literary point of view their importance is indisputable. In contrast, the works from the period after the *Postscript* have usually not been accorded the same quantity or quality of attention. . . . However, for the purpose of understanding SK's view of society and of the relationship between religion on the one hand and politics and culture on the other, it is this second half of SK's literary career which is more important.

2. Kant (1996, 63) writes in the conclusion of this essay,

> When nature has, under this hard shell, developed the seed for which she cares most tenderly—namely, the inclination and the vocation for *free thinking*—this works back upon the character of the people (who thereby become more and more capable of *acting freely*) and finally even on the principles of government, which finds it to its advantage to treat man, who is now *more than a machine*, in accord with his dignity.

3. Hegel quotes the first two and last two lines of a speech by Mephistopheles in Part I, Scene IV:

> Verachte nur Vernunft und Wissenschaft,
> Des Menschen allerhöchste Kraft . . .
> . . . und hätt' er sich auch nicht dem Teufel übergeben,
> er müßte doch zugrunde gehen! (Goethe 1963, 147)

4. In *Kierkegaard and Kant: The Hidden Debt*, Green (1992, 87) writes,

> For some scholars, to the extent that Kierkegaard recognizes a philosophical ethics at all, it is Kant's ethics. But he does so, they contend, only to reject it. Those who hold this view tend to believe that Kierkegaard's ethic is fundamentally religious . . .

5. For an interesting discussion of the link between weakness of will and procrastination, see Mark Kingwell's "'We Shall Look into it Tomorrow': Kierkegaard and the Art of Procrastination" (2013).

6. For further discussion of this point, see Philip L. Quinn's "Kierkegaard's Christian Ethics" (1998).

7. Jason Mahn's *Fortunate Fallibility: Kierkegaard and the Power of Sin* offers a theological reading of Kierkegaard's views concerning "the blessing of human fragility" (Mahn 2011, 51).

8. Haufniensis writes, "Hereditary sin is something present; it is sinfulness, and Adam is the only one in whom it was not found, since it came into being through him" (CA 26/SKS 4:333).

9. In contrast, Kant believes that there are postulates of practical reason (God, freedom, and immorality) that cannot be proven, but yet still ground ethics. For Kant, religion is beyond the limit of reason, but ethics is not beyond its limit—even if God, freedom, and immortality make ethics possible. Even more, reason has a tendency to reach beyond its bounds and so must be held in check.

> ... even the *assumption*- as made on behalf of the necessary practical employment of my reason- of *God*, *freedom*, and *immortality* is not permissible unless at the same time speculative reason be deprived of its pretensions to transcendent insight. For in order to arrive at such insight it must make use of principles which, in fact, extend only to objects of possible experience, and which, if also applied to what cannot be an object of experience, always really change this into an appearance, this rendering all *practical extension* of pure reason impossible. I have therefore found it necessary to deny *knowledge*, in order to make room for *faith*. (Kant 1929, 29)

10. Essays in *Kierkegaard After MacIntyre: Essays on Freedom, Narrative, and Virtue*, such as Marino's "The Place of Reason in Kierkegaard's Ethics" and Rudd's "Reason in Ethics: MacIntyre and Kierkegaard," challenge MacIntyre's reading of Kierkegaard, particularly on the issue of "criterionless choice." I believe Kierkegaard's emphasis is not on how one *decides* to become ethical, but how one *shows the decision* in real life.

11. Here Kierkegaard may be following the example of Johann Hamann who also questions the coherence of pure reason in his *Metacritique of the Purism of Reason*.

12. Kierkegaard even predicted this misreading of his work: "... they will probably bawl out that I do not know what comes next, that I know nothing about sociality. You fools!" (JP 5:363/SKS 20:86)

13. Kierkegaard's pseudonym, Anti-Climacus, writes, "... for truly to be a Christian certainly does not mean to be Christ (what blasphemy!) but means to be his imitator..." (PC 106/SKS 12:114).

14. Saez Tajafuerce cites Theodor W. Adorno, "On Kierkegaard's Doctrine of Love" in *Studies in Philosophy and Social Science*, vol. 8, 1940. pp. 413–429.

15. In the mentioned passage, Saez Tajafuerce writes only about the first imperative and thus the concepts of love and the neighbor. I also believe that the concept of imitation in the second imperative could likewise be included in an extension of her argument. Although Jesus' life contained a finite number of actions, the imitation of Christ is not meant to be a totally literal endeavor, but rather an attempt to do what Jesus *would* do; thus, the possibilities for imitation could be infinite.

Chapter Three

Language and Communication

If ethical reflection is meant to give way to ethical action in the second ethics, it is worth considering the compatibility of reflection's tool, language, with ethics. This compatibility may be judged in two ways: externally and internally. Language may have external compatibility with ethics if it has the ability to *describe* ethics, or in other words, provide an account of ethics from an external point of view. Language's internal compatibility has to do with language's role *within the activity* of ethics. In the case of the first ethics, language has both a valuable external and internal function. Language can sufficiently describe the content of the first ethics through the articulation of moral imperatives. Additionally, language is required within the activity of the first ethics when moral agents disclose the motivations and reasons for their actions. However, in the case of the second ethics, language's external and internal roles are deficient.

Language's successful description of the second ethics depends on 1) the proper or improper use of language, and 2) attributes belonging to language's own nature. Put another way, language's ability to describe the ethical ethics depends on the user of language employing it correctly, and on language itself being an adequate medium of communication.

In "Language and the Ethical in the Thought of Kierkegaard," Shin Ohara (1967b, 32) distinguishes between three ways to use language about what is real:[1] "We note three ways to treat actual reality: first, making the real into the unreal; making the unreal into the real; and the third, regarding the real as it is. Irony is an instance of the first type. Pretending to be better, being hypocritical, is the second. . . . Both hypocrisy and irony are possible relative to any expression, for the hypocrisy and irony lie not in the words but in their use." *How* language is used can determine whether it expresses irony, hypocrisy, or is a correct statement about reality.

Some philosophers of language maintain that there are certain rules, or conventions, that govern the use of language, and these rules usually contain a stipulation that language should preserve the truth. For example, H. Paul Grice (1990, 152) writes of "general conditions that . . . apply to conversation," among which are maxims to "try to make your contribution one that is true" and "do not say what you believe to be false." Without these rules, the simple act of conversation would be jeopardized and progress in science would be impossible. In these contexts, Kierkegaard concedes the importance of language: "a scientist . . . always needs to be reconciled to and be in reconciliation with language" (CA 184/Pap. V B 50).

Yet science is not the only context of language, and so hypocrisy and irony provide possibilities for language to achieve ends other than "regarding the real as it is." Kierkegaard, "the master of irony" (PV 66/SKS 16:47), frequently uses irony in his literary productions to counter what he considers to be the rampant hypocrisy of his age. This hypocrisy is due in great part to the misuse of religious language, a misuse intended to weaken its content so that its demands are not so strenuous or to give the appearance of piety.

> Another one of the disastrous results of Christendom's having become part of the established order is that the language has become meaningless or topsy-turvy . . . now in Christendom the expression: By the help of God's grace, it is not I who do it, it is God's grace—this has become a hackneyed phrase which everybody uses and consequently there is no opposition. Or this expression also comes to be understood as pretentious piety, because this grinding away at grace is a triviality, but when someone places special accent upon it, there he must want to be regarded as especially pious. The meaninglessness arises from the fact that the attackers use the same language. (JP 1:309–310/Pap. IX A 232)

If it is the case that the hypocritical use of religious language has rendered that language "meaningless," then language would certainly be challenged to describe accurately the Christian framework of the second ethics.[2]

A larger issue than language's misuse threatens language's ability to describe the second ethics, however. This issue does not involve language's proper usage, but rather involves its own nature. Ohara's (1967b, 3) essay "delineate[s] the functions of language for expressing the ethical: . . . its externalization, its universalization, the significance of abstraction, and the simplifications it produces." Each of these functions fails in some respect for the second ethics.

The first function of language is externalization, by which Ohara (1967b, 3) means "[l]anguage . . . externalizes the real into possibility and into ideality. . . . Both ethos and faith presented by language are only the externalized form of the real ethos and real faith with language as the medium. In either case, we have a translation." Certainly, there is an obvious distinction between a name and the object named, so there is a difference between ethics and faith "presented by language" and their "real" forms. Language is necessarily concerned with the outward, or external, since it involves a public exchange of concepts. As Paul Tillich (1952, 91) writes, "language is communal, not individual." Language is a "medium," a "translation," between two speakers; it serves as a bridge crossing between the understanding of members of a linguistic community. Yet, in contrast to language's outwardness, the second ethics is essentially inward. The second ethics' subject is the actual rather than the conceptual, and involves the private (as connected to the purely individual movement of faith) rather than the public. The distinction between the outward and the inward cannot be blurred without risking the substance of the ethical and religious. Kierkegaard's Climacus writes,

> Hegelian philosophy culminates in the thesis that the outer is the inner and the inner is the outer. With this, Hegel has finished. But this principle is essentially an esthetic-metaphysical principle, and in this way Hegelian philosophy is happily and safely finished without having anything to do with the ethical and the religious, or it finishes in a fraudulent manner by combining everything (also the ethical and the religious) in the esthetic-metaphysical. The ethical already establishes a kind of contrast-relation between the outer and the inner, inasmuch as it places the outer in the sphere of indifference . . . ethically the question is only about the inner. (CUP 1:296–7 fn/SKS 7:270)[3]

When language attempts to describe the second ethics, in its articulation of that which is essentially inward, language makes the actual into the merely possible, and therefore "dissolving the *esse* of actuality into *posse*" (CUP 1:358/SKS 7:327). Kierkegaard's Climacus writes,

> . . . existence-actuality cannot be communicated, and the subjective thinker has his own actuality in his own ethical existence. If actuality is to be understood by a third party, it must be understood as possibility, and a communicator who is conscious of this will therefore see to it, precisely in order to be oriented to existence, that his existence-communication is in the form of possibility. A production in the form of possibility places existing in it as close to the recipient as it is possible between one human being and another. (CUP 1:358/SKS 7:326)

The actuality of the ethical individual can only be viewed by another as possibility, and this is "as close" as a person can be to another's ethical existence. However, it is clear that ethical possibility is a weak substitute for ethical actuality: "From the ethical point of view, actuality is superior to possibility. The ethical specifically wants to annihilate the disinterestedness of possibility by making existing the infinite interest" (CUP 1:320/SKS 7:292). Language's function of externalization therefore prevents adequate description of the second ethics because it externalizes the second ethics' inwardness and thereby translates ethical actuality into mere ethical possibility.

Another function of language that stymies the description of the second ethics is universalization. Ohara (1967b, 6) points to Hegel as a proponent of this function, "For Hegel, even this 'This,' the 'Here,' and the 'Now,' the evacuations of particularity, become universals as soon as they are thought. Even the most elementary articulation of experience . . . is a conceptual reconstruction of experience." For Hegel, language, concept, and consciousness are interlocked; something that lies beyond the grasp of language is therefore beyond the grasp of thought. According to his view, truth particularly cannot be expressed. He writes in *Phenomenology of Spirit* that if we take any particular thing, like a specific piece of paper, its particularity cannot be stated; "If [someone] actually wanted to *say* 'this' bit of paper which they mean, if they wanted to *say* it, then this is impossible because the sensuous This that is meant *cannot be reached* by language, which belongs to consciousness, i.e. to that which is inherently universal" (Hegel 1977, 66). Nothing, if it is to be regarded as rational or meaningful, is inarticulable. The inarticulable is, for Hegel (1977, 66), "nothing else than the untrue, the irrational, what is merely meant." Only the universal can be "reached by language" and the particular cannot.

Hegel's views are not unique in the history of philosophy. Aspects of this view can be seen in Parmenides' metaphysical poem about what can be said and thought, as well as in the Logical Positivism movement, long after Hegel, which equated the meaningful with the verifiable. On the other hand, Johann Hamann (2007, 212), a significant influence on Kierkegaard,[4] offers an interesting objection to the claim that language is pure concept by stating that language has aesthetic and bodily qualities (i.e. words are heard and seen), and that feeling and thinking are united in our human experience: "The sensibility and the understanding arise as two stems of human knowledge from One common root."

In no other work of Kierkegaard is the tension between the universal and the particular so explicit as it is in *Fear and Trembling*. Its pseudonym, literally John of silence, writes of Abraham's necessary silence about his willingness to sacrifice Isaac. For Abraham, speech would violate his private responsibility to God and draw him into the realm of the universal and the ethical (of the first ethics). In *Fear and Trembling*, it is language's function of universalization that poses a threat to the religious, because the thrusting out of the essentially inward into the public and universal domain of the outward is what reduces the knight of faith into the mere ethical hero. It is important to keep in mind that the ethics discussed in *Fear and Trembling* is the first ethics, the ethics that arises out of and demands the universal. However, the second ethics, as a religious ethics, requires the particular—the particular individual in their particular relationship with God in a particular moment. The universalization of language does not just cause the knight of faith to disappear, it also causes the authentically ethical to disappear as well. Seeing beyond Johannes de silentio's link between the universal and ethical to Kierkegaard's own more complete view, Jacques Derrida (1995, 60) offers an interpretation of *Fear and Trembling* that draws to the surface the conflict between the universal and the authentically ethical:

> Just as no one can die in my place, no one can make a decision, what we call 'a decision,' in my place. But as soon as one speaks, as soon as one enters the medium of language, one loses that very singularity. One therefore loses the possibility of deciding or the right to decide. Thus every decision would, fundamentally, remain at the same time solitary, secret, and silent. Speaking relieves us, Kierkegaard notes, for it 'translates' into the general. The first effect or first designation of language therefore involves depriving me of, or delivering me from, my singularity.

The loss of singularity, of particularity, means the loss of the authentically ethical. The ethical action (specifically, love of neighbor and imitation of Christ), which lies at the core of the second ethics, is made by the fully responsible and infinitely interested individual who does not seek relief from this responsibility by being translated "into the general." Such a translation is equivalent to the abdication of responsibility from the individual to disinterested, non-invested outsiders.

The third function of language discussed by Ohara is abstraction. Abstraction happens when language "make[s] static that reality which is still in the process of becoming" (Ohara 1967b, 8). The operative distinction involved with this function of language is between the relatively fixed nature of language and the absolutely unfixed nature of reality in which the second ethics participates. Ohara (1967b, 8) writes, "Kierkegaard's point is that words are self-identical over a period of time while the reality is not." Language arguably has an evolution and a movement of its own, but its movement does not immediately track the movement of reality. In creating succinct encapsulations of reality in the form of statements, language does not present a fully accurate account of reality that involves constant change. It is the movement of reality that interests Kierkegaard: "Kierkegaard wants resolutely to avoid turning the world into a frozen *eidos*, stilling its movement, arresting its play, and thereby allaying our fears. He wants to stay open to the *ébranler*, the wavering and fluctuating, and to keep ready for the fear and trembling, the anxiety by which the existing individual is shaken" (Caputo 1988, 12). Language does not mirror reality's "wavering and fluctuating," but instead catches a snap-shot of reality from the position of the observer. One of Kafka's parables[5] describes a philosopher who interrupts a children's game with a spinning top. In order to take a closer look at the top, he grasps it in his hand and thereby stops the top's movement. Like the spinning top whose essence consists in its movement and ceases to function once held in hand, reality ceases to be what it is when it is fixed to a point in time by language. Through the application of language, the temporality of reality is distorted; it no longer exists in a constantly moving present, but becomes pinned to a moment in the past.

> Language indeed mediates between the present and the past, and contains in a conceptual way the reality of the present in its retrospective character. . . . To describe the present is to foreclose on the present process of the object; it is to give definition and a kind of permanence to an unfinishable object. In using language, we abstract from the present by omitting the vitality and the élan of the object. (Ohara 1967b, 8)

The second ethics "is never observing, but always accusing, judging, acting" (CA 22/SKS 4:330), and as such, moves with the motion of present reality. Unlike the first ethics which relies on the imperatives of ideality (like Kant's categorical imperative), the second ethics centers itself in reality and sets into motion the activity of ethical striving. It is ethical striving, the constant movement demanded by the second ethics, that conflicts with the motionlessness of language's abstraction.

The fourth and final function of language discussed by Ohara is simplification. Ohara (1967b, 11) writes, "to find words and to think a thing is to apprehend it in the mode of simplicity and possibility." Language's "context and . . . intention can be complex" (Ohara 1967b, 11), but language's basic role of assigning names and situating them within a system of grammar is nonetheless an act of simplifying language's object.

In the last chapter, the second ethics' tasks were defined as love for the neighbor and imitation of Christ. These two activities are particularly elusive to describe because, in the act of reducing them to words or ascribing a definition for them, they do not retain their richness and complexity. The acts of love required by the second ethics are "*essentially* inexhaustible" (WL 3/SKS 9:11) and "the neighbor" as the object of the second ethics is "all people" (WL 19/SKS 9:27). The difficulty posed by language's simplification is that it creates a finite expression in place of an infinite task (infinite works of love) directed toward an infinite object (infinite neighbors).

Yet language's simplification does not only reduce what may be meant by love and neighbor. It also gives a false impression of what is involved in carrying out the second ethics. The ethical striving required by the second ethics is a striving in and of existence, one that is strenuous and one that applies to all. The attempt to apply language to it fails to capture its movement and entirety, and it also distracts the abstract thinker from the immediate task of carrying out its requirements. Even if one were to try with language to capture the complexity of the ethical task, Kierkegaard could critique this activity as yet another form of ethical evasion. The person attempting this would be "inattentive to the task of actually *living* ethically" (Compaijen and Vos 2019, 70).

The four, above-mentioned functions of language (externalization, universalization, abstraction, and simplification) do not represent an exhaustive account. Rather, these four functions of language have been singled out because they prevent language from satisfactorily describing the second ethics. Language fails to provide a comprehensive and precise description of the second ethics because these functions cannot retain what is central to the second ethics, namely, inwardness, particularity, movement, and complexity. Yet, the source of language's failure lies deeper than in just these four functions. The profound mismatch of language and the second ethics stems from an original tension between ideality and reality. In *Johannes Climacus*, the tension creates contradiction: "Immediacy is reality; language is ideality; consciousness is a contradiction. The moment I make a statement about reality, contradiction is present, for what I say is ideality" (PF 168/SKS 15:55) The oppositions highlighted by the four functions of language (external vs. internal, universal vs. particular, static vs. movement, simple vs. complex) arise out of this original tension between the reality of existence and the ideality of language.

The tension between the reality of existence and the ideality of language gives rise to a problem for language's external use of describing the second ethics. It also prevents language's internal use of enacting and communicating the second ethics. As mentioned earlier in this chapter, language's compatibility with the second ethics does not only depend on language's ability to describe the second ethics from the *outside*, but also its ability to work *inside* the actual activity of the second ethics. In other words, language's external use is how language can *speak* about the content of the second ethics; language's internal use is how language *participates* in the second ethics. Language's internal use is judged by how well it aids in communicating and carrying out the imperatives of the second ethics.

Kierkegaard wrote that the misuse of language is a "sin . . . [which] is undoubtedly as prevalent as the sins of flesh and blood, possibly even more widespread, embracing all men" (JP 3:12/Pap. XI-2 A 128). He wrote of three kinds of misuse of language: 1) hypocrisy, 2) the depreciation or emptying of words, and 3) using language as a form of ethical or religious evasion. In the first case, one uses language to puff oneself up to appear greater than one is. In the second case, one uses language to deflate meanings of words so that they no longer pose a difficult or strenuous demand. In the third case, one chatters and gossips to fill time and distract oneself from one's tasks.

Hypocrisy is one form of language's misuse because the hypocrite uses language in order to proclaim certain values or commitments while their life expresses a different set of values and commitments. Language is the medium the hypocrite uses to paint a pleasing public portrait of themself that is at odds with their true self. Kierkegaard counted "speakers, teachers, [and] professors" as those who typically engage in hypocrisy by putting on the "disguises of language" (JP 3:12/Pap. XI-2 A 128). Kierkegaard demanded their frisking, just as "the police thoroughly frisk suspicious persons," by "ordering them to be silent, saying: Shut up, and let us see what your life expresses, for once let this be the speaker who says who you are" (JP 3:12/Pap. XI-2 A 128). These professors are no less than cannibals, Kierkegaard goes on to say, "in the fact they live off others who have been slain, persecuted, and maltreated for the truth" (JP 3:649/Pap. XI-1 A 100). Even more, he said they are worse than cannibals because they protract their cannibalism (whereas normal cannibals do their job quickly) and because they befriend those they cannibalize (whereas normal cannibals don't feign friendship with their prey). "[C]annibals shall enter the kingdom of God before the clergy and professors" (JP 3:649/Pap. XI-1 A 100), Kierkegaard wrote, adding "were there no hell, it would have to be made in order to punish the professors, whose crime is such that it can scarcely be punished in this world" (JP 3:653/Pap. XI-1 A 473). In these harsh passages, Kierkegaard calls professors out from behind their books into the open and demanding the kind of accountability for consistency between words that express values and actions that truly reveal them, an accountability that applies to all. He wrote, "We have invented scholarship in order to evade . . . we protect ourselves by making it seems as if it [God's will] were very difficult to understand and that therefore we . . . study and investigate etc., that is, we protect ourselves by hiding behind big books" (JP 3:657/Pap. XI-2 A 376).

The depreciation of words is another form of language's misuse. Kierkegaard wrote, for example, how the word "grace" has been devalued through its misuse in Christendom. He claimed it had become a "hackneyed phrase" because everyone, those sincere and insincere, used it to create an appearance of piety. He wrote, "The meaninglessness [of the word] arises from the fact that the attackers use the same language" (JP 1:310/Pap. IX A 232). Kierkegaard identified overuse and lack of opposition as causes for the word's devaluation. If everyone uses a word carelessly, including those whose lives oppose its genuine meaning, then the word loses its potency. This depreciation is not a benign mistake of linguistic usage, but is an ethically suspect act. It is a form of moral evasion when the existential demands of the words are removed from their meaning. This is particularly the case, Kierkegaard thinks, in the case of the words "Christianity" and "Christian." The depreciation of these words comes from overuse and lack of opposition in the context of Christendom, but it also seems to come about purposely in order to avoid the difficulty presented by the real meanings of these words.

> For what is Christendom? It is this indulgence continued from generation to generation, whereby first of all a little bit is knocked off of what it means to call oneself a Christian, and the next generation knocks off a little of what had been knocked off of the already discounted price, etc.—all through the misuse of language, by continuing to use the highest and most decisive expressions while continually investing them with less and less meaning, continually committing themselves less and less to what the words say. (JP 3:13/Pap. XI-2 A 128)

The devaluation or "discounting" of "the highest and most decisive expressions" is a way of getting oneself off the hook by not having to commit oneself "to what the words say."

Chatter is the third form of language's misuse. Kierkegaard defined chatter as "the annulment of the passionate disjunction between being silent and speaking" (TA 97/SKS 8:93). Chatter can be gossip, small talk, or speaking for its own sake. Chatter both thwarts action through the distraction of talking and covers the chatterer's uncomfortable "emptiness" (TA 98/SKS 8:93).

Kierkegaard's criticism of language is not simply meant to expose and scold its misuse; he also believed that language cannot fully express what is most ethically meaningful. In some notes for potential lectures on "The Dialectic of Ethical and Ethico-Religious Communication" that are included in his *Papirer*,[6] Kierkegaard writes that communication consists of "four parts: (1) the OBJECT, (2) the COMMUNICATOR, (3), the RECEIVER, (4) the COMMUNICATION" (JP 1:281/Pap. VIII-2 B 83). In relation to these four parts, Kierkegaard makes three distinctions: the first distinction concerns the communication's object, the second distinction concerns the communication, and the third distinction concerns the relation between the communicator and the receiver. These three distinctions outline the elemental differences between what Kierkegaard calls "the communication of knowledge" (*Videns Meddelelse*) and "the communication of capability" (*Kunnens Meddelelse*).

The first distinction Kierkegaard draws concerns communication's object. When the emphasis falls on the communication's object, the communication is a communication of knowledge, and when there is no object in the communication, the communication is a communication of capability. In a communication of knowledge, the object is "either knowledge about something" (JP 1:270/Pap. VIII-2 B 81), which includes "the so-called knowledge about knowledge" (JP 1:270/ Pap. VIII-2 B 81) since this is "knowledge *about something*" (JP 1:270/ Pap. VIII-2 B 81), or it is self-knowledge. In this kind of communication, the object has a superior status compared to the other parts of the communication: "This is apparent from the lowest empirical knowledge to the highest. It is always 'the object' which is reflected upon. 'The communicator,' 'the receiver,' 'the communication' are completely in the background" (JP 1:283/Pap. VIII-2 B 85).

In contrast to a communication of knowledge, a communication of capability has no object. Kierkegaard makes a division of capabilities along the three spheres of existence; according to him, there is an "esthetic capability," an "ethical capability," and a "religious capability" (JP 1:281/Pap. VIII-2 B 83). He writes that for the "ethical capability or oughtness capability . . . there is unconditionally no object" (JP 1:281/Pap. VIII-2 B 83). Here, the ethical capability's lack of object is contrasted with religious capability's initial object. Religious capability has "an object insofar as there is at first a communication of knowledge" (JP 1:281/Pap. VIII-2 B 83); this knowledge is about Christianity and "must certainly be communicated in advance. But it is only a preliminary" (JP 1:289/Pap. VIII-2 B 85). In contrast, Kierkegaard believes that ethical capability has no object since everyone already knows the content of the ethical: "Every human being knows the ethical" (JP 1:271/Pap. VIII-2 B 81). For Kierkegaard, like Socrates,[7] the ethical is not a matter of speculation or theorizing, but is something that already resides within the individual. Since the ethical is already known by all, Kierkegaard concludes that the ethical cannot be considered to have an object that can be communicated; "Let us now make an experiment and assume that there is an object or a knowledge which we all have. What would the implications be for the dialectical in communication? From this it would follow: (1) the object drops out, for if we all know it, one person cannot communicate it to another. . . ." (JP 1:271/Pap. VIII-2 B 81). Because the communication of ethical capability has "unconditionally no object," the futility of language becomes clear. Language is a "medium" or "translation" (Ohara 1967b, 3) of an object from one person to another; without such an object to mediate or translate, language cannot perform.

The second distinction Kierkegaard draws concerns "the communication" and this distinction has two parts: (1) "when 'the communication' is reflected upon . . . in the sense of 'the medium' (JP 1:281/Pap. VIII-2 B 83) and, (2) "when the 'communication' is reflected upon" (JP 1:282/Pap. VIII-2 B 83). The first part of the distinction, reflection upon "the communication" as a medium, highlights the difference between a communication in the medium of possibility and a communication in the medium of actuality. The second part of the distinction, reflection upon "communication" itself, highlights the difference between direct and indirect communication.

Kierkegaard writes that "all communication of knowledge is in the medium of imagination (possibility)" (JP 1:282/Pap. VIII-2 B 83). This is not to say that the object of a communication of knowledge is something that is created by the imagination, but rather that it communicates its object as a possibility instead of as an actuality. A communication of knowledge is mediated in the realm of ideas. So, although a communication of knowledge may be *about* reality, it is nevertheless not the reality itself. Kierkegaard illustrates the difference between the actuality of existence and the possibility of language through the example of a swimming lesson. Speaking about the swimming strokes on dry land is one thing, while really doing the strokes in the water is another. In speaking about the strokes outside of the water, the strokes are mere possibility. In the water, the strokes are actuality.[8] As in the case of the swimmer whose swimming lesson is not in water, a communication of knowledge in the wrong context can lead to false learning. Kierkegaard notes there is something "deceptive in instructing young people in the medium of imagination or fantasy; whereas everything looks just the opposite in the medium of actuality" (JP 1:275/Pap. VIII-2 B 81).[9]

In contrast to a communication of knowledge in "the medium of imagination or fantasy" (JP 1:282/Pap. VIII-2 B 83), a communication of capability "is in the medium of actuality" (JP 1:282/Pap. VIII-2 B 83). Here, actuality is understood as "the existential reduplication of what is said" (JP 1:286/Pap. VIII-2 B 85). Ethical capability must be "unconditionally" (JP 1:282/Pap. VIII-2 B 83) communicated in the medium of actuality, and its proper communication is "recognizable by the fact that the communicator himself is and always strives to be that which he communicates" (JP 1:275/Pap. VIII-2 B 81). The successful communication of ethical capability depends on the match between *what* is being communicated and *how* it is being communicated; thus "the situation" of the communicator is something "essential" (JP 1:286/Pap. VIII-2 B 85) to the communication.

> ... the communication in the ethical can be given only in actuality, in such a way that the communicator or teacher himself exists in it and in the situation of actuality, is himself in the situation of actuality that which he teaches. When someone instructs in ataraxy—from a platform—it is not ethically true. No, the situation must be such that he himself demonstrates ataraxy simultaneously as he instructs in ataraxy. For example, if someone is instructing in ataraxy while surrounded by a crowd of people who are insulting him—this is a genuine situation of actuality. (JP 1:275/Pap. VIII-2 B 81)

Again, it is plain to see that language's role in the communication of ethical capability is problematic. A communication of ethical capability depends on corresponding actions, or the reduplication in actuality of that which is being communicated. A legitimate communication of ethical capability requires one to be ethical, not to merely talk about the ethical. Merely talking about the ethical transforms it from an ontological state of the subject to a conceptual object. Consequently, talking about the ethical is not an ethical communication. Kierkegaard writes, "... the ethical cannot be taught didactically, for to teach it didactically is to communicate it unethically" (JP 1:286/Pap. VIII-2 B 85).

How something is communicated, as opposed to *what* is communicated, is also relevant to the second part of the distinction, reflection upon "the communication" itself. Here, Kierkegaard differentiates between direct and indirect communication; he writes, "all communication of knowledge is direct communication" (JP 1:282/Pap. VIII-2 B 83), whereas "all communication of capability is indirect communication" (JP 1:282/Pap. VIII-2 B 83), and again, this is unconditionally the case for ethical capability.

Kierkegaard describes direct communication as that in which the communicator directly delivers the communication's object to the receiver; ". . . this is direct communication, I do not reduplicate, I do not execute what I am lecturing about, I am not what I am saying, I do not give the truth I am presenting the truest form so that I am existentially that which is spoken. I talk *about* it" (JP 1:298/Pap. VIII-2 B 88). Direct communication is appropriate when the communication is about empirical fact, for example. However, Kierkegaard was more concerned with direct communication's inappropriate application, as in cases when it is applied to a communication of capability. Perhaps it is true that "direct communication indeed makes life far easier" (PV 249/SKS 23:472), but for Kierkegaard, who believed that "the noble nature is inspired only by what is difficult" (JP 1:303/Pap. VIII-2 B 88), direct communication's ease does not give it an advantage. When a communication of ethical capability is communicated directly, the communicator evades responsibility; "The minute I use direct communication, the truth loses in intensity and I to some extent escape martyrdom: is this permissible, is this not deceiving God?" (PV 300/SKS 21:45). When direct communication treats the communication of capability as a communication of knowledge, not only is what is being communicated weakened (for example, by simplifying the complex, universalizing the particular, abstracting the actual, and externalizing the internal), but it also indicts the user of direct communication of falsely trying to make things easier. If the aim of the second ethics is earnest ethical striving, then an evasion or mitigation of ethical responsibility only serves as evidence against the agent's earnestness.

Indirect communication, however, is the appropriate method for a communication of capability. Kierkegaard gives three reasons why this is the case:

> The communicator always dares influence only indirectly, (1) because he must always express that he himself is not a master-teacher but an apprentice and that God, on the other hand, is his and every man's master-teacher, (2) because he must express that the receiver himself knows it, (3) because ethically the task is precisely this—that every man comes to stand alone in the God-relationship. (JP 1:273/Pap. VIII-2 B 81)

The first reason concerns the issue of authority. For Kierkegaard, false authority leads to hypocrisy and puts the communicator and receiver into an improper relation. Kierkegaard saw a misunderstanding about authority as one of the failures of his generation: "What is the basic confusion in modern life it if is not this—that in every communication of truth they consider man to be the authority rather than that God is the authority, especially in ethical-religious communication" (JP 1:298/Pap. VIII-2 B 88). The second reason for indirect communication concerns the maieutic method, which is, according to Kierkegaard, the right way to teach the ethical; "When in reflection upon the communication the receiver is reflected upon, then we have ethical communication. The maieutic. The communicator disappears, as it were, makes himself serve only to help the other become" (JP 1:307/Pap. VIII-2 B 89). In general terms, Kierkegaard interprets the maieutic method as a particular relationship between a teacher and pupil in which the teacher does not give information to, but draws knowledge out of, the pupil. Kierkegaard associates the maieutic method with Socrates' role as a "midwife" to the ideas of others. Kierkegaard writes, ". . . Socrates remained true to himself and artistically exemplified what he had understood. He was and continued to be a midwife . . . because he perceived that this relation is the highest relation a human being can have to another" (PF 10/SKS 4:220). The third reason for indirect communication centers on the necessity for individual ethical choice. The second ethics, as described in the previous chapter, is a Christian ethics that requires a private and individual movement of faith.

On the surface, it seems like a couple of inconsistencies emerge from these three reasons for indirect communication. First, there seems to be an inconsistency between the authority of the communicator and the maieutic method. If the communicator really disappears into the background leaving the receiver alone, what is the value of the communication if it is not really from the communicator? Another related inconsistency appears to arise between the maieutic method and the necessity of ethical individuality since the communicator is attempting to help someone who essentially cannot be helped by another. However, these inconsistencies may be resolved through a clarification of the ways in which indirect communication may be produced.

In a section entitled "The Impossibility of Direct Communication" in *Practice in Christianity*, Kierkegaard's Anti-Climacus writes that indirect communication "can be produced in two ways" (PC 133/SKS 12:137). The first way is through "double-reflection" (PC 133/SKS 12:137), or through the deliberate attempt to tie the communication into a "dialectical knot" (PC 133/SKS 12:137) which makes it into a sort of puzzle that the receiver has to solve for himself. An indirect communication taking this form could include using pseudonyms, parables, aphorisms, and other such literary devices.[10] In these instances, the communicator's maieutic task is to present the puzzle and to disappear once it is presented. Therefore, the communicator's disappearance is a part of the puzzle; the communicator does not lose authority, but gives the appearance of it. The receiver, then, alone as an individual, may or may not solve the puzzle. The receiver, in effect, retains their necessary individuality, but the communicator's presence lingers in the maieutic presentation.

The second way to produce indirect communication, Anti-Climacus writes, is when the communicator, not the communication, is the puzzle. First, the communicator must be the reduplication of the communication within existence, but must also be a "being . . . based in reflection" (PC 134/SKS 12:139). Christ is the perfect example of this kind of indirect communication because he "is a sign, the sign of contradiction; he is unrecognizable—therefore any direct communication is impossible" (PC 134/SKS 12:139). Human attempts at indirect communication, no matter how strenuous, will merely be imperfect attempts. Whereas the first kind of indirect communication concerns the communication itself (as presenting a puzzle), the second kind concerns the credibility of the communicator (who is the puzzle). In the second kind, the communicator may well possess the authority to communicate, but this authority remains hidden from the receiver. For example, in the case of Christ, the receiver has to decide whether to believe in his authority. Kierkegaard writes,

> If someone says directly: I am God; the Father and I are one, this is a direct communication. But if the person who says it, the communicator, is this individual human being, an individual human being just like others, then this communication is not quite entirely direct, because it is not entirely direct that an individual human being should be God . . . it becomes indirect communication; it confronts you with a choice: whether you will believe him or not. (PC 134/SKS 12:139)

In both kinds of indirect communication, (1) "double-reflection" and (2) "reduplication" by a communicator who is a "being . . . based in reflection" (PC 134/SKS 12:139), the work of deciphering the communication (making sense of it and deciding whether or not to believe it) belongs to the receiver. Language may have some role in indirect communication, but it is secondary to action.

The third distinction Kierkegaard draws in his notes on "The Dialectic of Ethical and Ethico-Religious Communication" concerns the relation of the communicator and the receiver. One can determine what kind of capability is being communicated by determining whether the emphasis is either on the communicator or receiver, or both equally. If it is equally on both communicator and receiver, then it is a communication of aesthetic capability. When the emphasis is on the communicator, it is a communication of religious capability.[11] But when the emphasis falls mainly on the receiver, it is a communication of ethical capability. This heightening of the role of the receiver is critical to the maieutic method: "To stand—by another's help alone—and—To stand alone—by another's help . . . the latter is the maieutic relationship . . . the maieutic's help is hidden" (JP 1:280/Pap. VIII-2 B 82). In teaching the ethical, the maieutic method does not depend on the efficacy of language, but on the communicator's presentation of the communication, their subsequent attempt to disappear from view, and the receiver's understanding of being able to do the ethical tasks independently from the (human) communicator.

Despite the many deficiencies of language outlined in this chapter (its improper use, the opposition between its four functions and the nature of the second ethics, and its failure to be a communication of capability), language is still regarded as an ethical tool. In fact, Ohara does not view the apparent deficiencies in languages four functions as deficiencies at all, but rather as positive functions between language and ethics. This interpretation, however, stems from a failure to differentiate between the first and second ethics, evinced in the following sentence: "Language for Kierkegaard is . . . the medium of the conceptual and, therefore, the ethical" (Ohara 1967b, 2–3). Ohara (1967b, 25) argues that language is "indispensable" and, as a way of connecting with others, is ethical: "Man might not need language for receiving divine revelation or other insights, but man does need language for communicating with fellow human beings. Language is thus indispensable, if not to fulfill the *amor fati* of man, also for the sake of an ethicality which seeks communication with others. To use language is, therefore, highly ethical." The recognition that language, fallible and sometimes unreliable, is our instrument is often followed by a sense of resignation. Language, however imperfect, is what we've been given to use. However, Kierkegaard presents us with another possibility, another form of communication that can complement, and perhaps surpass, the work done by language with regard to the second ethics. This other possibility is the subject of the next chapter.

NOTES

1. Heidegger (1971, 192) writes something similar: ". . . human expression is always a presentation and representation of the real and unreal."

2. Wittgenstein (1980, 39) proposes a solution for language's failure due to frequent misuse: take the language out of circulation, give it a cleaning, and bring it back. ("Man muß manchmal einen Ausdruck aus der Sprache herausziehen, ihn zum Reinigen geben, -und kann ihn dann wieder in den Verkehr einführen.") Although a clever idea, it assumes a control of language we likely don't enjoy without major collective effort.

3. In *Concluding Unscientific Postscript*, Climacus does not differentiate between the first and second ethics, so when he speaks of the inwardness of the ethical in this quotation, he is speaking less of the inwardness required by faith than of a particular ethical inwardness that is based on personal motivations for action: "The outer as material for action is a matter of indifference, because the purpose is what is ethically accentuated; the outcome as the externality of action is unimportant, because the purpose is what is ethically accentuated . . ." (CUP 1:297 fn/SKS 7:270). This is consistent with a Kantian view that emphasizes the motivations for actions rather than their consequences as the basis of moral content. Climacus goes on to say that "The religious definitely establishes the contrast between the outer and the inner . . ." (CUP 1:297 fn/SKS 7:270), so we may conclude that for a religious ethics, such as the second ethics, the distinction between the outer and the inner is relevant. Additionally, in *Practice in Christianity*, Anti-Climacus writes, "The first condition for becoming a Christian is to become unconditionally turned inward. Infinitely turned inward . . ." (PC 225/SKS 12:219).

4. For more on Hamman's influence on Kierkegaard, see my article "Hamann: Sharing Style and Thesis: Kierkegaard's Appropriation of Hamann's Work" in *Kierkegaard and His German Contemporaries: Tome III: Literature and Aesthetics*. Edited by Jon Stewart. Burlington, VT: Ashgate Publishing Limited, 2008.

5. Kafka's parable titled "The Top" contrasts the philosopher's search for a static object of investigation against the moving nature of reality. Kafka (1971, 444) writes of the philosopher that "he believed that the understanding of any detail, that of a spinning top, for instance, was sufficient for the understanding of all things." Of course, when he grasps after the spinning top, he stops its motion and is left with a static, uninteresting object, a "silly piece of wood in his hand" (Kafka 1971, 444). This parable also suggests that children, in their active and playful engagement with their game and each other, are the true philosophers.

6. The value of these notes on communication cannot be overstated. Kierkegaard sees a need to clarify what he specifically meant by communication:

> . . . if an author has his own distinctive conception of communication, if all his distinctiveness and the reality of his historical significance are perhaps focused precisely in this, well, then it will be a long-drawn-out affair—O, school of patience. Before there can be any mention of understanding something of what he has communicated, one must first understand him in his distinctive dialectic of communication and in this light understand everything which one understands. And this, his distinctive dialectic of communication, he cannot, however, communicate in the traditional dialectic of communication. (JP 1:264/Pap. VIII-1 A 466)

There is no doubt that some of Kierkegaard's greatest intellectual contributions are his views on *how* the genuinely meaningful can be communicated. Given his emphasis on the method of communication, these notes are a critical key for understanding his ideas.

7. Kierkegaard is not an advocate of anamnesis, like the kind presented in Plato's *Meno*. But like Socrates, Kierkegaard believes that individuals already know the ethical and so therefore do not need to invent it from scratch. Kierkegaard writes, "The communication here implies luring the ethical out of the individual, because it is in the individual" (JP 1:269/Pap. VIII-2 B 81).

8. Kierkegaard contrasts our preference for talk over action in this example: "As far as 'actuality' is concerned, almost all men have a kind of fear of water. They want the teacher to be related to them as the swimming instructor who in a safe and 'quiet hour' explains the motions of swimming to them; but when he says: Let us now dive in, they say: No thanks" (JP 1:287/Pap. VIII-2 B 85).

9. Communication in the medium of possibility does not only carry the potential for misleading young people, but Kierkegaard also sees its prevalence in the philosophies of his age as their major shortcoming. *Johannes Climacus* explores what can happen if one tries to take a philosophical motto, like "everything should be doubted," as something more than a slogan to parrot.

10. Kierkegaard's own success with this form of communication is impressive, and has even sparked interpretive controversy. For example, Joakim Garff (1999, 9) advanced a deconstructive interpretation of Kierkegaard, including Kierkegaard's "meta-text," *The Point of View On My Work as an Author*, in which he set about "reading Kierkegaard with Kierkegaard against Kierkegaard." His interpretation takes Kierkegaard's various manipulations of his reader very seriously:

> The [Kierkegaardian] texts themselves have the character of a picture puzzle or a cunning labyrinth, found as they are in secret, whether in the innermost parts of a chest-of-drawers under sudden attack or at the bottom of the Søborg Lake, where they have rested for a century before being dragged to the surface by the help of a sophisticated, underwater instrument. This confusing multiplicity of voices, pens, positions, and literary teases is not only found in the aesthetic writings but is also encountered in the more philosophical sections of the collected works . . . , and thus requires an enormous vigilance on the part of the reader, a bifocal vision, which not

only should take a hold of *what* Kierkegaard writes but also envelop the text and contemplate *how* he writes what he writes. (Garff 1999, 10)

Others, like Sylvia Walsh (1999, 8), who writes, "Who is to judge that Kierkegaard lacked that inwardness and truth? . . . Perhaps it is Garff, then, not Kierkegaard, who wants to keep Kierkegaard 'interesting' by deconstructing and distorting his explanations into fiction," are skeptical of such a deconstructive interpretation. Whatever the solution here, the debate itself shows the great interpretive task Kierkegaard leaves to the reader.

11. In terms of religious capability, this communicator is to be understood as Christ/God: "There remains only one communicator: God" (JP 1:272/Pap. VIII-2 B 81).

Chapter Four

Silence

Silence may be interpreted as either a positive or negative phenomenon. As a negative phenomenon, silence is the absence of something else, where the "something else" can be, but is not limited to sound, music, language, and movement. Absence is what is meant by silence's negativity. In this sense, silence is determined by something else's non-existence. Silence *is* because something else *is not*. As a negative phenomenon, silence's relevance depends on its tension and juxtaposition with its opposite.

When silence is regarded as a negative phenomenon, it usually corresponds with a negative ethical judgment of silence. This is due to a commonly held view that silence is the absence of what is usually valued positive and good. The description of silence as absence, then, typically entails an evaluation of silence as something that needs to be fixed or resolved. In "The Machine Stops: Silence in the Metaphor of Malfunction," Ron Scollon (1985, 26) writes, "The normal state of the machine is thought of as a steady hum or buzz, with hesitation or silences indicating trouble, difficulty, missing cogs, and so forth." Silence is not only seen as being negative in the case of malfunctioning machinery (an apt metaphor in a post-industrial age), but is also linked to a malfunctioning culture by thinkers such as Jean-Paul Sartre and George Steiner. For these writers, silence indicates a social and/or political rupture that needs to be mended by language. In his essay titled "What Is Literature?" that gives a response to the question "Why Write?," Sartre (1988, 66) maintains that literature is an expression of freedom. He writes that in our roles as author and reader ". . . both of us bear the responsibility for the universe." For Sartre (1988, 52), the value of silence comes from its status as the place where the reader begins to produce meaning out of words, to ". . . hold on to, the words and sentences which he awakens." Even if silence is an initial meeting point for the author and reader, both the author's task (writing) and the reader's task (awakening the meanings) depend on the production of words. Steiner, too, wishes for silence to be avoided through vibrant public discourse about literature.

> Because the community of traditional values is splintered, because words themselves have been twisted and cheapened, because the classic forms of statement and metaphor are yielding to complex, transitional modes, the art of reading, of true literacy, must be reconstituted. It is the task of literary criticism to help us read as total human beings, by example of precision, fear, and delight. Compared to the art of creation, that task is secondary. But it has never counted more. With it, creation itself may fall upon silence. (Steiner 1967, 11)

There are numerous other instances of critiques of silence's absence of language, from the "silence is death" campaign for AIDS awareness to the calls for ending silence as a way to resist and undermine patriarchy, white supremacy, and other systems of oppression.

It is interesting to note that silence's opposite, language, may also be viewed as either a positive or negative phenomenon. Whereas language's status as a positive phenomenon is widely recognized, and is clearly supported in Sartre's and Steiner's work, language's status as a negative phenomenon is less familiar, but may be seen in such movements as mysticism and deconstructionism. To give one example, Maurice Blanchot (1999, 381) describes language as a negative phenomenon: "Language can only begin with the void; no fullness, no certainty can ever speak; something essential is lacking in anyone who expresses himself. Negation is tied to language. When I first begin, I do not speak in order to say something, rather a nothing demands to speak, nothing speaks, nothing finds its being in speech and the being of speech is nothing." Like Kierkegaard's views about how the ideality of language blocks out the actuality of existence, Blanchot (1999, 379) describes language's negativity as the absence, or annulling of, being; "For me to be able to say, 'This woman' I must somehow take her flesh and blood reality away from her, cause her to be absent, annihilate her. The word gives me the being, but it gives it to me deprived of being. The word is the absence of that being. . . ."

Silence need not be regarded only as a negative phenomenon, however. Viewed as positive, silence is important in its own right. As such, silence is independent and meaningful in itself; it is not the mere absence of something else, but is itself a presence.[1] When silence is interpreted in this way, it is permitted to communicate in a manner that is unique to it. Silence, like language, can convey meaning and is therefore another form of communication. Paolo Scarpi (1987, 21) writes in "The Eloquence of Silence: Aspects of a Power without Words" that, ". . . one cannot help but communicate, in the same way as one speaks of 'eloquent silences.' Here one is already within the realms of what silence implicitly evokes: communication. . . . However, if it is a means of communicating, it is opposed to what daily experience recognizes as a particular and perspicuous manifestation of communication: the word." Peter Fenves (1993, 145) writes something similar in *Chatter: Language and History in Kierkegaard*: "Communication cannot *not* take place. . . . Even noncommunication—whether as silence, muteness, or total passivity—is a negative mode of communication, which, however, remains a matter of communication." Fenve's view, in particular, shows the difficulty in maintaining the position that silence is only a negative phenomenon when he writes that silence as a "noncommunication" somehow "remains a matter of communication." When silence is considered seriously, it is impossible to overlook its communicative power. Positively viewed, silence still indicates an absence, but this absence need not be considered something that should be filled in or corrected. On the contrary, the purposeful creation of silence allows for a valuable alternative mode of communication: exemplification, or expression through action. When silence is a negative phenomenon, it marks the absence of something, whether it is language, music, sound, or movement (as mentioned earlier); but when silence is a positive phenomenon, it is in exclusive juxtaposition with language. When positive, silence competes with language as a method of communication. In this shift away from language, change happens not to what is communicated, but to how it is communicated. The emphasis moves from *saying* to *doing*.

The boundary between saying and doing, however, is not always sharp. Speaking, itself, is a form of doing that does not just involve semantics and grammar, but also includes a variety of activities like having intentions, pronouncing words, and producing various effects in listeners. As John Searle (1990, 115) writes,

> In a typical speech situation involving a speaker, a hearer, and an utterance by a speaker, there are many kind of acts associated with the speaker's utterance. The speaker will characteristically have moved his jaw and tongue and made noises . . . he will also have performed acts within the class which includes making statements, asking questions, issuing commands, giving reports, greeting, and warning.

Reading and writing are still other obvious physical activities associated with language. Language's production, therefore, involves actions; *saying* involves some sorts of *doing*.[2] Likewise, some sorts of doing require a specific sort of saying. There are instances such as saying "I promise x" or "I am saying x" where the utterance of these is part of the actual activity of promising or saying.[3] These cases are unique in the sense that their truth values as actions depend exclusively on the production of language. One may argue that the truth of 'I promise x' depends not at all upon the actual fulfillment of promise x, but only upon the utterance of these words: "I promise x." In these types of instances, like that of promising or saying, there is equivalence between saying and doing, because the doing is related specifically to the production of language. Other sorts of doing may also involve saying. For example, Kierkegaard considered his book, *Works of Love*, to be an actual act of love.[4] Here, as in many other cases, even common ones like saying "I love you," the activity of loving does not exclude language, but rather requires it.

Although saying and doing may not be easily untangled, there remains a relevant difference between the production of language (speaking about x) and the production of action (doing x). In Plato's *Ion*, Socrates points out that Ion may recite excellent verses about a chariot race, yet still may know nothing about how to handle a horse. Moreover, Ion may be the best reciter of Homer in all Greece, but yet may not be able to write poetry, nor judge a poem's worth. Ion's particular talent is that he is able to speak about something well, and this indeed is an activity (namely, reciting), yet Socrates does not consider this activity a form of art or science.[5] Socrates says that Ion's talent must be a "divine gift" (Plato 1997, 942) passed from the gods through Homer to Ion. Socrates concludes that this "divine gift" is the authoritative source for his words (presuming he isn't cheating),[6] as opposed to an artist or craftsman who finds an authoritative source in his practical experience. Whether or not a "divine gift" is the actual origin of Ion's skill, Socrates calls attention to the fundamental difference between *speaking about x* and *doing x*. When someone *speaks about x* (such as Ion speaks about driving a chariot), there is a distance between the subject who speaks and the object about which he speaks. For Socrates, this distance is filled by the gods in Ion's case; the gods have direct knowledge of the subject which they give as a "gift" to Ion. Even if the notion of a "divine gift" is not rationally acceptable, it is still the case that Ion's authority over the subject is second-hand, because direct knowledge of the subject did not originate in him. Ion's subject is external to him since it is merely an object of discourse. When someone *does x* (such as the charioteer driving the chariot), there is no distance between the subject (the charioteer) and the object (chariot driving). The subject and the object relate in actuality. Additionally, the subject relates to the object in such a way that they have authority over and responsibility for the object. Both *saying* and *doing* convey information about the object (i.e., they are methods of communication), yet *doing* requires the subject to bear authority and responsibility in a way that *saying* does not necessarily require. Socrates asks Ion who is a better judge about the quality of Homer's verses about a chariot race: a charioteer or Ion himself. Ion must, and does, answer a charioteer.[7] Ion speaks about the charioteer's activity; the charioteer embodies it and *exemplifies*, taking on all its risk and reward.

Exemplification is a method of communication distinguished as a creative embodiment, a conscious doing of what which is to be conveyed. As such, exemplification often presents an artistic challenge. The composer John Cage (1973, ix) writes, "My intention has been, often, to say what I had to say in a way that would exemplify it; that would, conceivably, permit the listener to experience what I had to say rather than just hear about it." The production of language also presents artistic challenges, such as finding correct wording, rhythm, and the meaningful creation of clarity or ambiguity. The artistic challenge inherent in exemplification is of an altogether different degree. The artistic challenge facing the user of language is primarily stylistic; the artistic challenge facing the user of action is stylistic *and* ontological. Exemplification entails activity related to being because the exemplifier is supposed to *be* or *bring into being* that which is communicated. The person who uses action by exemplifying does not stand and point at the subject from a distance, but rather unites with the subject by associating with it in actuality. Cage's listeners are to "experience" what he intends to communicate, and Socrates' charioteer participates in charioteering. Therefore, silence emerges as a method of communication in its own right when saying ends and doing begins. Although silence indicates the absence of language, it does not necessarily follow that it also indicates the absence of communication. On the contrary, silence may be viewed as a positive phenomenon when it facilitates communication by exemplification and action.

KIERKEGAARDIAN SILENCE

Kierkegaard recognizes silence as both a positive and negative phenomenon. He views it as the end-point and subsequent absence of language, and as the condition for communication in the form of exemplification. For Kierkegaard, the concept of silence (*Tavshed*) is in inverse relation to language, as opposed to sound, music, or anything else. Kierkegaard uses another word to describe the absence of sound, music, etc.; this he calls quietness (*Stilhed*). He uses the word 'quietness' to denote the silence of nature and the silence of holy acts. Take, for example, the following two passages: "But the person who truly made up his mind, that person is quiet. And this is also like changing one's clothes, to take off everything that is noisy since it is empty, in order, hidden in quietness, to become disclosed. This quietness is the simple solemnity of the holy act" (UDVS 20/SKS 8:135), and "When the traveler leaves the noisy main highway and comes to the quiet places, he feels as if he had to talk with himself (for the quietness is soul-stirring!), feels as if he had to say what lies hidden in the depth of his soul" (UDVS 20/SKS 8:135). Silence, on the other hand, is not a state in which the individual rests, like quietness or peacefulness, but rather it is an action, a concealment.

In viewing silence as a negative phenomenon, Kierkegaard's de silentio writes that silence may be both the "demonic," the absence of language that closes off the individual from any form of communication, and the "divine," the absence of language that draws the individual and God together: "If I go further, I always run up against the paradox, the divine and the demonic, for silence is both. Silence is the demon's trap, and the more that is silenced, the more terrible the demon, but silence is also divinity's mutual understanding with the single individual" (FT 88/SKS 4:178). The absence of language can tend in two completely different directions: the demonic and the divine.

The category of the demonic corresponds to what Kierkegaard's called inclosing reserve (*Indesluttethed*), or the complete shutting off of the individual from the world and God.

> Generally, a more metaphysical expression is used for evil, namely, the negative. The ethical expression for it, when the effect is observed in the individual, is precisely this inclosing reserve. The demonic does not close itself up with something, but closes itself up within itself, and in this lies what is profound about existence, precisely that unfreedom makes itself a prisoner. Freedom is always *communicerende* [communicating] (it does no harm even to take into consideration the religious significance of the word); unfreedom becomes more and more inclosed [*indesluttet*] and does not want communication. (CA 124/SKS 4:425)

The demonic is ethically unacceptable isolation caused by the absence of communication. The individual who exists within the demonic category falls into uncommunicative withdrawal, rather than freely expressive disclosure. Ettore Rocca (2000, 78) describes demonic silence as "obstinacy" in "the despairing individual [who] yearns desperately to be himself, that abstract self created in his own mind; he wants to recreate himself and to recreate the world on the basis of his own desperate vitality. It is the pinnacle of the rejection of otherness, because he thinks he can ground his own self in self-sufficiency; it is a titanic struggle with the world." This is the situation of maximum despair as described in *The Sickness Unto Death*, and therefore, for Kierkegaard, demonic silence should be avoided. Not only is demonic silence a negative phenomenon, in the sense that it is the absence of communication, but it is also negatively valued as an expression of disconnection and unfreedom. This kind of silence must be remedied by the production of language; "Inclosing reserve is precisely muteness. Language, the word, is precisely what saves, what saves the individual from the empty abstraction of inclosing reserve" (CA 124/SKS 4:426).

Demonic silence corresponds to a conception of sin understood not as disobedience to laws or commands, but rather understood as a turning away from God and inward onto oneself. It is a conception of sin as closing oneself off from relationship. The systematic theologian Matt Jenson (2006, 3), writes that according to this view, "sin . . . is not *merely* pride, but the willful re-direction of attention and love from God to the human self apart from God which results in alienation from God and the fracturing of human society." The harm caused by this curving inward is therefore two-fold. One harm is to human society and therefore is highly visible. Think of all of the perversions of our relationships that come from obsessive self-focus: environmental degradation from anthropocentrism; economic disparity from the pursuit of unfettered financial self-interest; all forms of discrimination like sexism, racism, ableism, ageism, xenophobia, and so on that comes from the exclusive orientation "of attention and love . . . to the human self." It's worth noting that some secular moral theories, like Hobbes's social contract and Ayn Rand's egoism, take self-interest as a first principle that most accurately describes who we are once we strip away all the rules, institutions, and social conditioning that hold this impulse in check. In addition to the first harm caused to society, the second harm caused is to one's own self. This harm is less visible, but as Kierkegaard's pseudonym Anti-Climacus warns in *The Sickness Unto Death* it is no less dangerous. This book catalogues the various forms of despair as ways in which we relate improperly to ourselves and to our creator. The deepest form of despair comes from a refusal to recognize oneself as created by God and the corresponding insistence on self-creation. The Lutheran understanding of this alienation from God is that it ultimately shuts out the possibility of love. The inward curving of the self blinds us from help that could be offered from the outside. Think of unfortunate Narcissus who is blind to anything but his own image in the reflecting pool.

Like demonic silence, divine silence is a negative phenomenon because it also signifies the absence of language. Kierkegaard's de silentio writes, "The demonic has the same quality as the divine, namely, that the single individual is able to enter into absolute relation to it" (FT 97/SKS 4:186). The single individual is in "absolute relation" to the demonic and divine because nothing external interrupts the relation. All external communication is completely cut off. In spite of sharing this similarity with demonic silence, divine silence is positively valued by Kierkegaard. Divine silence refers to the silence of the individual engaged in an absolute and private relationship with God. Divine silence is not caused by willful disobedience or rejection of others, but rather by the ineffable character of God and God's relationship with creation. Unlike demonic silence in which the individual breaks with the world because of a purposeful choice not to communicate with others in order to create an artificial self-determined world, divine silence causes the individual to break with the world not due to choice, but due to the insurmountable impossibility of communication. In Kierkegaard's theology, God is paradox, and as such lies beyond any attempt at explanation and comprehension. Language, as a human-based and fallible tool, cannot penetrate the mystery of God. In contrast to the demonic in which there is a radical misrelation between the single individual and God, divine silence is "divinity's mutual understanding with the individual" (FT 88/SKS 4:178). Divine silence indicates, for Kierkegaard, a proper relation between the single individual and God; "Every human being who knows how to keep silence becomes a divine child, for in silence there is concentration upon his divine origin; he who speaks remains a human being" (JP 4:98/SKS 18:154).

George Steiner (1994, xxi) writes that "Kierkegaard is a celebrant of inward withdrawal, of absolute silence." Steiner is correct in connecting inward withdrawal and silence, for as Kierkegaard writes, "Silence is inwardness" (TA 97/SKS 8:93). However, Steiner's statement also reflects a common tendency by Kierkegaard's interpreters to overlook the complexity of Kierkegaard's views on silence. Silence, for Kierkegaard, does not simply indicate inward withdrawal. It is not merely the absence of communication that results when an individual closes in completely on their own self (the demonic) or closes in completely with God (the divine). Silence, when a positive phenomenon, also holds an important communicative role within Kierkegaard's work, particularly in the communication of capability. In the previous chapter, it was stated that a communication of capability, as a form of indirect communication, may be done in two ways: double-reflection and reduplication. Both of these methods of indirect communication require the communicator to be silent.

Kierkegaard writes,

> Indirect communication can be an art of communication in redoubling the communication. . . . This is what some pseudonymous writers are accustomed to calling the double-reflection of communication. For example, it is indirect communication to place jest and earnestness together in such a way that the composite is a dialectical knot—and then to be a nobody oneself. If anyone wants to have anything to do with this kind of communication, he will have to untie the knot himself. (PC 133/SKS 12:137)

This passage describes three particular qualities of a double-reflection: 1) the communication is in the form of a puzzle, or a "dialectical knot," 2) the receiver of the communication is to "untie the knot himself" (this is, if he wants to participate in the communication), and 3) the communicator is to disappear, or become a "nobody." The double-reflection is a puzzle in which the communicator places "qualitative opposites in a unity," for example, by placing "jest and earnestness together," bringing "attack and defense into a unity," or by presenting faith so that "the most orthodox sees it as a defense of the faith and that the atheist sees it as an attack" (PC 133/SKS 12:137). The receiver, then, goes about finding a meaning for what has been communicated. He is to untangle the "qualitative opposites" that have been intertwined "in a unity." This gives the reflection its doubled nature: "the first is the reflection in which the communication is made, and the second is that in which it is recaptured" (JP 1:274/Pap. VIII-2 B 81). The receiver cannot passively absorb the communication, but rather must actively seek a meaning for it. Finally, there is the communicator who is to become "a nobody . . . an absentee, an objective something, a nonperson" (PC 133/SKS 12:137).

Double-reflection is not the absence of language, but the purposeful use of language that turns language against itself. It amounts to silence on the part of the communicator. The communicator presents opposites together so that one asks whether they are jesting or in earnest, attacking or defending, orthodox or atheist. The silence of the communicator consists in the absence of their clear choice between the "qualitative opposites." For Kierkegaard, the absence of the communicator's choice turns them invisible or non-existent. In *Either/Or*, Judge William writes that "if a person could continually keep himself on the spear tip of the moment of choice," then he would "stop being a human being" (EO 2:163/SKS 3:160). The communicator of a double-reflection communicates this feeling of being on the "spear tip." This is not to say that the communicator does not truly make a choice or hold an opinion about the "qualitative opposites" which they present in union, but rather that they withhold or are silent about their choice in a double-reflection. On the one hand, the communicator uses the communication to remain silent and conceal their view; on the other hand, the receiver, in selecting a meaning, discloses their view. The meaning of the communication belongs solely to the receiver who creates it, and in this task of assigning meaning, the receiver shows who they are. Kierkegaard imagines the communicator to play the role of ". . . an ingenious secret agent who with the aid of this communication finds out which is which, who is the believer, who the atheist, because this is disclosed when they form a judgment about what is presented, which is neither attack nor defense" (PC 133–4/SKS 12:139). The communicator is hidden and silent; the receiver chooses a meaning and is revealed.

In a communication as double-reflection, the communicator's silence is a positive phenomenon because it communicates through initiating the activity of the receiver. The object communicated, the unison of "qualitative opposites," serves to pose for the receiver a choice to be made between the opposites, or even something new altogether (as in the case of *Either/Or* when the opposites of the aesthetic and the ethical are both unsatisfactory). In a double-reflection, the emphasis is not on the communicator *saying*, but is placed on the receiver *doing* (creating a meaning by separating and making a judgment about the opposites).

The second way Kierkegaard believes a communication of capability can be expressed is through reduplication. As opposed to a double-reflection in which the object communicated presents a choice for the reader, in a communication as reduplication, the communicator is the exemplifier. To reduplicate (*Reduplikationen*) is "to be what one teaches" (JP 1:287/Pap. VIII-2 B 85).

> "Actuality" is the existential reduplication of what is said. To teach in actuality that the truth is ridiculed, etc. . . . , means to teach it as one ridiculed and

> scoffed at himself. To teach poverty in actuality means to teach it as one who is himself poor (profiting—in the sense of advancing a science, an art, not in the sense of having profit from it). To that extent all instruction ends in a kind of silence; for when I existentially express it, it is not necessary for my speaking to be audible. (JP 1:286/Pap. VIII-2 B 85)

Reduplication is similar to a double-reflection in that it presents the receiver with a choice. However, these two methods of indirect communication differ in how the choice is presented. In a double-reflection, the "qualitative opposites," or competing choices, are presented in unison by the communicator. In contrast, reduplication involves the communicator reduplicating, or exemplifying, only one position within actuality. In a double-reflection, the communicator conceals their own self like "an ingenious secret agent" (PC 133/SKS 12:139) in order to reveal the receiver's choice; in reduplication, the communicator is revealed. The communicator is not revealed through language, but through action. Therefore, the communicator who reduplicates is essentially silent. The communicator may speak, but speaking is subordinated to the higher task of being what is communicated. Kierkegaard writes, "Only the person who can remain essentially silent can speak essentially, can act essentially" (TA 97/ SKS 8:93).

Silence is also a positive phenomenon in reduplication. The silence of the communicator allows for another method of communication than language; they communicate the object by demonstrating it through being.

> The distinguishing characteristic in life is not what is said but how it is said. . . . *How* is there not the esthetic, the rhetorical, whether spoken in flowery language or in a simple style, whether with euphonious organ tones or with a scratchy voice, whether dryly and unemotionally or with tears in the eyes, etc.—no, the distinction is whether one *speaks* or whether one *acts* by speaking, whether one uses the voice, facial expression, arm gestures, single word thrice, perhaps ten times underscored, etc., for emphasis in order to make an impression or whether one uses his life, his existence, every hour of his day, sacrifices, etc., for emphasis. This emphasis is the elevated emphasis which transforms what is spoken into something entirely different even though a speaker says literally the same thing. (JP 1:317–8/Pap. X-2 A 466)

Reduplication is inherently connected to silence. In contrast, language, particularly in the form of chatter, diverts attention from the needed action. In *Two Ages*, Kierkegaard writes,

> What is it to chatter? It is the annulment of the passionate disjunction between being silent and speaking. Only the person who can remain essentially silent can speak essentially, can act essentially. Silence is inwardness. Chattering gets ahead of essential speaking and giving utterance to reflection has a weakening effect on action by getting ahead of it. But the person who can speak essentially because he is able to keep silent will not have a profusion of things

to speak about but one thing only, and he will find time to speak and to keep silent. (TA 97/SKS 9:93)

The use of language may also show a lack of resolution or commitment. Kierkegaard criticizes the replacement of action with indecisive discussion:

> Although all of them, when they are supposed to act, discuss it with 'the others' and all that—they all nevertheless say depreciatively of someone: He went and discussed it beforehand with 'the others.' Consequently they betray themselves, betray their awareness of the fact that authentic intensive actions spring from an individual and from silence. (JP 4:100/SKS 24:212)

Kierkegaard asserts that silence is the "fundamental tone" (FSE 49/SKS 13:75) for action. He acknowledges a direct correspondence between silence and the capacity to act: "Silence and the capacity to act correspond to each other completely; silence is the measure of the capacity to act; a person never has more capacity to act than he has silence" (WA 56/SKS 11:62).

NOTES

1. An example of this view is found in Bernard P. Dauenhauer's (1980, vii) work, which states, "Silence is a complex, positive phenomenon. It is not the mere absence of something else."

2. John Stuart Mill's *On Liberty* famously investigates what kinds of uses of language constitute harms and whether we are justified in censoring speech. For a contemporary take on this issue, see, for example: McGowan, Mary Kate. *Just Words: On Speech and Hidden Harm*. New York: Oxford University Press, 2019.

3. J.L. Austin (1990, 109) writes, "For when we say 'I promise that . . .' we do perform an act of promising—we give a promise. What we do not do is to report on somebody's performing an act of promising—in particular, we do not report on somebody's use of the expression 'I promise.' We actually do use it and do the promising."

4. Kierkegaard writes, "I dare to call this book a work of love" (WL 455/Pap. VIII-2 B 73).

5. Socrates says to Ion: "Anyone can tell that you are powerless to speak about Homer on the basis of knowledge or mastery. Because if your ability came by mastery, you would be able to speak about all the other poets as well. Look, there is an art of poetry as a whole, isn't there?" (Plato 1997, 940).

6. Socrates asks, "So choose, how do you want us to think of you—as a *man* who does wrong, or as someone *divine*?" (Plato 1997, 949). To avoid the unfortunate alternative of Ion being a fraud, Socrates poses the possibility of a divine source for his skill.

7. "Socrates: But doesn't Homer speak about professional subjects in many places, and say a great deal? Chariot driving, for example. . . . Then who will know better whether or not Homer speaks beautifully and well in the lines you quoted? You, or a charioteer?
Ion: A charioteer." (Plato 1997, 944–45).

Chapter Five

Ethical Silence

The various pieces of this argument until this point—the distinction between the first and second ethics, the communicative limits of language, and the correspondence between silence and action—can be gathered together to construct a new perspective on Kierkegaard's views on the relationship of silence and the ethical. Silence has a necessary presence in the religious sphere, and therefore it follows that the second ethics, with its definite connection with the religious, also invites silence. However, a distinguishing difference between the silence of the religious and the silence of the second ethics has to do with its necessity; whereas religious silence is necessary because of the ineffable nature of God and the privacy of the relationship between God and the individual, the silence of the second ethics is elective, as a conscious choice not to speak. The religious presents a subject about which one *cannot* speak. The second ethics presents a subject about which one *should not* speak. The second ethics, a specifically Christian ethics, sets forth the two imperatives to imitate Christ and to love the neighbor. To fulfill these tasks, Kierkegaard writes that silence is not only ethically permissible, but even advisable.

SILENCE AND THE IMPERATIVE TO IMITATE CHRIST

Kierkegaard articulates the second ethics' imperative to imitate Christ primarily in *Practice in Christianity*: "Christ's life here on earth is the paradigm; I and every Christian are to strive to model our lives in likeness to it" (PC 107/SKS 12:115) Kierkegaard does not see an inconsistency between Luther's emphasis on justification through faith alone and the imperative to imitate Christ. He interprets Luther's *Sola Fide* as a corrective to the errors of the pre-Reformation Church which displayed "exaggeration with regard to works" (FSE 193/SKS 16:240). "But let us not forget," writes Kierkegaard, "Luther did not therefore abolish imitation. . . . He affirmed imitation in the direction of witnessing to the truth and voluntarily exposed himself there to dangers enough . . . and although Luther was not put to death, his life was nevertheless, humanly speaking, a sacrificed life, a life sacrificed to witnessing to the truth" (FSE 193/SKS 16:239). Although Luther is concerned about the error of empty works without faith, Kierkegaard sees an equal error of empty faith without works. He believes that Luther's corrective had overcorrected in his own age so that "modern philosophy" (PC 141/SKS 12:145) and "official Christianity" (TM 129/SKS 13:174) weaken Christianity by ignoring this imperative. Without this imperative, Christianity becomes mere a set of teachings that one believes or a doctrine that one accepts. The relation between the believer and Christianity, therefore, becomes a poetical relation rather than an existential relation.

> . . . official Christianity is a falsification that solemnly assures that Christianity is something else entirely, solemnly declaims against atheism, and by means of this covers up that it is itself *making* Christianity into poetry and abolishing the imitation of Christ, so that one relates oneself to the prototype only through the imagination but oneself lives in totally other categories, which amounts to relating oneself poetically to Christianity or to changing it into poetry, no more binding than poetry is. Finally one discards the prototype altogether and lets what one is, mediocrity, be regarded more or less as the ideal. (TM 129/SKS 13:174)

Kierkegaard insists that a poetical relation with Christianity is deficient. Christ's life should not be esteemed and admired as a distant and intangible ideal far removed from the reality of one's life. Kierkegaard's Anti-Climacus writes that this would be an incorrect view of what Christianity really endorses: "contemporaneity with Christ" (PC 62/SKS 12:74), who is the absolute and the prototype of the way one should live. Having "contemporaneity with Christ" means to put Christ's life into the reality of one's own present life by emulating it. Christ's significance extends beyond his historical existence. His life "stands alone by itself, outside history" (PC 64/SKS 12:76) and is the paradigm in whose footsteps the Christian is to follow; "Christ came into the world with the purpose of saving the world, also with the purpose—this in turn is implicit in his first purpose—of being *the prototype*, of leaving footprints for the person who wanted to join him, who then might become an *imitator*" (PC 238/SKS 12:232). Therefore, the relation between the individual and Christianity is intended to be existential, rather than poetic. The imperative to imitate Christ is not an invitation to admire Christ's life and sayings from a distance, while at the same time conducting life "in totally other categories" (TM 129/SKS 13:174). Rather, the imperative to imitate Christ is to direct the whole course of one's existence.

Kierkegaard writes that Christ is the ultimate paradox of Christianity in which the divine and human are united. The paradox of Christ presents a "situation [which] no human understanding can endure" (PC 116/SKS 12:123). This breakdown of understanding leaves one confronted with a choice to believe that Christ is both human and God, or to take offense at this paradox. Anti-Climacus tells us that Christ makes offense possible in three ways: 1) he is a man who claims to be God, or "loftiness" (PC 82/SKS 12:92), 2) he is God who claims to be a man, or "lowliness" (PC 82/SKS 12:92), and 3) he comes into collision with the established order. The first two sources of offense come about through the paradoxical pairing of the divine and human in the "God-man" (PC 81/SKS 12:92), and are therefore impossible for humans to imitate. However, the third source of offense originates from Christ's actions in the world, and consequently may be imitated.

The "established order" connotes many things for Kierkegaard, most notably, the universal, objectivity, secularity, complacency, and convention. He writes, "The deification of the established order, however, is the smug invention of the lazy, secular human mentality that wants to settle down and fancy that now there is a total peace and security, now we have achieved the highest" (PC 88/SKS 12:97). He maintains that those who worship and serve the established order, among whom he counts Hegel, are in "perpetual revolt, the continual mutiny against God" (PC 88/SKS 12:97); "Why has Hegel made conscience and the state of conscience in the single individual 'a form of evil' (see *Rechts-Philosophie*)? Why? Because he deified the established order" (PC 87/SKS 12:96). Christ collides with the established order because he represents singularity, subjectivity, piety, perpetual striving, and inwardness. The conflict between Christ and the established order is most perceptible through their opposing answers to the question that Kierkegaard considers in much of his work, beginning with *Fear and Trembling*: "Is the single individual higher than the universal?" (PC 85/SKS 12:94). The established order answers no, while Christ answers yes.

> . . . Christ . . . emphasizes inwardness in contrast to empty outwardness, a teacher who transforms outwardness into inwardness. This is the collision, a collision that appears again and again in Christendom; to put it briefly, it is the collision of pietism with the established order. . . . The established order . . . always insists on being the objective, higher than each and every individual, than subjectivity. The moment when an individual is unwilling to subordinate himself to the established order or indeed even questions its being true, yes, charges it with being untruth, whereas he declares that he himself is in the truth and of the truth, declares that the truth lies specifically in inwardness—then there is the collision. (PC 86/SKS 12:95)

When Christ, or the imitator of Christ, emphasizes their singularity over the demands of the universal, then "the established order poses the question:

Who does this individual think he is? Does he perhaps think that he is God or that he has an immediate relation to God, or at least that he is more than a human being?" (PC 86/SKS 12:95). The established order mistakenly interprets the individual's singularity as pride, revealing an underlying misunderstanding. This misunderstanding creates the conditions for offense. "Every time a witness to the truth transforms truth into inwardness (and this is the essential activity of the witness to the truth), every time a genius internalizes the true in an original way—then the established order will in fact be offended at him" (PC 87/SKS 12:96). What the established order perceives as pride, the Christian perceives as humility. The individual who imitates Christ's inwardness is not transcending humanness, but rather recognizes human imperfection and identifies as a "sufferer:"

> The question is: does a human being have the right to that extent to take sides with God against man; is it not treason toward men and forwardness toward God? Here the life of Christ is not illuminating because he himself was God. But if a person is to remain among men, we get no further than the religiosity of human sympathy. Here as everywhere I see only one way out: if a person is going to cling to God in this way, it must not be in the direct superexcellence of humanness but inversely through the misery of being subordinated under the universally human, put outside it, and thus as a sufferer constrained to relate himself absolutely to God as his only possibility. (JP 1:312–3/SKS 21:279)

When the imitator of Christ is set apart from others in a position of singularity in an absolute relation to God, their goal is obedience, but their actions are interpreted by others as pride and thereby inspire offense. The temptation, then, for the imitator of Christ is to resolve this misunderstanding by means of communication. To speak would release the imitator of Christ from the burden of their separation from and misunderstanding with others. In numerous instances, most notably in his private journals, Kierkegaard writes about his own difficulty with being misunderstood. For example, he writes, "I, too, would like to make myself comprehensible. . . . But I dare not, for then I defraud the idea" (JP 5:315/Pap. VII-1 A 98).[1] By speaking, the individual has the "power to gain happiness in the world, to win men" (JP 1:298/Pap. VIII-2 B 88), but would also thereby be "giving truth a less true form" (JP 1:298/Pap. VIII-2 B 88). Speaking in this case would compound the misunderstanding by giving the impression that the absolute or one's relation with the absolute are comprehensible. However, this would give a false impression because the absolute is paradoxical in essence. It is precisely the absolute's paradoxical nature that makes faith and offense possible. The attempt to clarify the absolute by speaking provides relief from the alienation from others, but in removing offense, it also removes faith. If direct communication is used, ". . . then Christianity is abolished, has become something easy, a superficial something that neither wounds nor heals deeply enough; it has become the false invention of purely human compassion that forgets the infinite qualitative difference between God and man" (PC 140/SKS 12:144). The "infinite qualitative difference between God and man" which makes Christ's identity as both God and man is the fundamental paradox presented by Christianity which results in the necessary (i.e., non-elective) silence of the religious sphere. Therefore, speaking about the absolute or one's relations with the absolute not only exacerbates misunderstanding in others, but it also weakens one's faith; "Talking about one's God-relationship is an emptying that weakens" (JP 4:100/SKS 26:314a).

Yet the choice of the individual of whether or not to speak in order to clear up the misunderstanding with others is both a religious and ethical choice because it involves not only the individual's relation with the absolute, but also their relation with other humans. In Kierkegaard's earlier works, such as *Fear and Trembling*, the choice is presented as binary; either one chooses God or one chooses the world. However, once Kierkegaard begins to develop his ideas about the second ethics in his later writings, the choice becomes one between an authentic relation with God *and* the world, or a false relation with God *and* the world. Inwardness, then, does not exclusively describe a closing-off from the world, but may also be descriptive of the state required for a particular sort of spiritual maturation that includes participation with and in the world. Through inwardness, one matures religiously, and also ethically. The question the later Kierkegaard asks is:

> Are you now living in such a way that you are aware of being a single individual and thereby aware of your eternal responsibility before God; are you living in such a way that this awareness can acquire the time and stillness and liberty of action to penetrate your life relationships? You are not asked to withdraw from life, from an honorable occupation, from a happy domestic life—on the contrary, that awareness will support and transfigure and illuminate your conduct in the relationships of your life. (UDVS 137/SKS 8:236)

Silence's connection with inwardness is obviously clear given that "silence is inwardness" (TA 97/SKS 8:93). The shift from the universal to the particular, from objectivity to subjectivity, from outwardness to inwardness, is a shift from language to silence. But understood as the condition for religious and ethical maturity, inwardness does not indicate the total absence of language nor the end of associations with others. Instead, Kierkegaard views inwardness as the foundation for authentic speech and action. He writes, "Only the person who can remain essentially silent can speak essentially, can act essentially" (TA 97/SKS 8:93). The silence of inwardness, then, may lead to alienation from the world, but does not also therefore lead to a complete divorce from it. In imitating Christ's inwardness, by opposing the established order, one makes offense and alienation possible, but correct imitation also involves "essential" or authentic participation in the world.

For Kierkegaard, Christ's perfection consists in how he lives his life. It is not merely that Christ speaks the truth, but that he is the truth. In this sense, Christ represents for Kierkegaard the perfect exemplifier of communication of capability.

> ... Come here to me, all you who labor and are burdened. This he says, and those who lived with him saw and see that there truly is not the slightest thing in his way of life that contradicts it. *With the silent and veracious eloquence of action, his life expresses—even if he had never said these words*[2] —his life expresses: Come here to me, all you who labor and are burdened. He stands by his word or he himself is his word; he is what he says—in this sense, too, he is the Word. (PC 14/SKS 12:24)

Christ, as *Logos*, communicates meaning (the "Word") through his being with such clarity that it is redundant for him to speak with language (". . . his life expresses—even if he had never said these words. . . ."). Although it is clear that Christ's words have significance, Kierkegaard wishes to draw attention to the communicative value of Christ's actions. Christ communicates "with the silent and veracious eloquence of silence." The imitator is to do this as well.

> ... [Christ] said something like this: Venture a decisive act; then we can begin. What does this mean? It means that one does not become a Christian by hearing something about Christianity, by reading something about it, by thinking about it, or, while Christ was living, by seeing him once in a while or by going and staring at him all day long. No, a *setting (situation)* is required—venture a decisive act; the proof does not precede but follows, is in and with the imitation that follows Christ. (FSE 191/SKS 16:238)

The "decisive act," rather than the exercises of language (hearing, reading, thinking, discussing) defines authentic contemporaneity with Christ, i.e. really being a Christian.

The incompatibility between action and language is two-fold: first, the production of language can be a distraction from making a "decisive act," and second, whereas action demonstrates faith, language may serve to demonstrate doubt. Excessive and extraneous language functions as a distraction when its noise drowns out significant and meaningful communication.

> ... create silence! Ah, everything is noisy; and just as a strong drink is said to stir the blood, so everything in our day, even the most insignificant project, even the most empty communication, is designed merely to jolt the senses or to stir up the masses, the crowd, the public, noise! And man, this clever fellow, seems to have become sleepless in order to invent ever new instruments to

> increase noise, to spread noise and insignificance with the greatest possible haste and on the greatest possible scale. Yes, everything is soon turned upside down: communication is indeed soon brought to its lowest point with regard to meaning, and simultaneously the means of communication are indeed brought to their highest with regard to speedy and overall circulation; for what is publicized with such hot haste and, on the other hand, what has greater circulation than—rubbish! Oh, create silence! (FSE 47–8/SKS 13:74–75)

It is hard to believe that this is written prior to the advent of the information and internet age, in which "hot haste" is brought to a whole new level. Kierkegaard seems to be addressing our current century, even more than the one in which he lived. Communication is "brought to its lowest point" through the superabundance of words and the speed at which they now are exchanged. Quality gives way to sheer quantity of words, making it ever more difficult to find kernels of truth.

Language can also be a distraction when the individual is occupied with speaking rather than doing. Language can trap the individual in contemplation of all the great possibilities ahead, rather than actually doing the task at hand.

> Only all too soon one's own experience and experience with others teach how far the lives of most people are from what a human life ought to be. All have their great moments, see themselves in the magic mirror of possibility that hope holds before them while desire flatters, but they speedily forget the vision in the everyday. Or perhaps they utter enthusiastic words, 'for the tongue is a little member and boasts of great things'—but by loudly proclaiming what ought to be practiced in silence the talk takes the enthusiasm in vain, and the inspired words are quickly forgotten in the trivialities of life; it is forgotten that such words were said about his person; it is forgotten that it was he himself who said them. (UDVS 31/SKS 8:145)

The use of language as a distraction from the execution of the "decisive act" may be caused by more than a simple avoidance of action, since it may mask a more serious underlying condition of doubt. One may speak enthusiastically about the actions one plans to do, but the focus on proclaiming them, rather than doing them, evinces a lack of resolve. In "Silence in the Myth: Psychoanalytical Observations," Alberto Schön (1987, 16–17) writes, "So the omnipotent 'temptation' can perhaps be expressed by the formula: destructive silence= to wish to think the unthinkable, whilst, for mature silence= the fundamental words have already been said and accepted." Schön identifies a possible meaning of silence: "the fundamental words have already been said and accepted." Acceptance is key to this particular meaning of silence. From this perspective, the use of language is symptomatic of lingering uncertainty and lack of resolution. Alternatively, silence indicates that the time for debate and decision is over, and language can no longer be used to convince or persuade because a conclusion has been reached. There is a danger here of course if one were to insist that debates are fruitless and decisions are cemented, particularly when we know that humans are fallible creatures whose ideas should be open to constant revision and scrutiny. Religious faith and our universal knowledge of the ethical, according to Kierkegaard, present interesting border cases, however, because debate and public scrutiny do not apply to them. This is the central disturbing conundrum of *Fear and Trembling*: Abraham has decided to follow God's command, and so is he a knight of faith or a monster? Schön's particular meaning of silence recalls the crucial distinction between speaking about x and doing x. For Kierkegaard, it is doing x that ultimately matters because it is one's actions, rather than words, that display the true conviction that one holds. Translating one's conviction into action is "the only demonstration" of having it, whereas merely stating or thinking it leaves the so-called conviction open to potential rejection because it remains as mere possibility among other options.

Kierkegaard calls the mismatch between one's words and actions "double-mindedness" (*Tvesindethed*).

> Or is it not double-mindedness to think one has a conviction that one contradicts in action? Or is it not truly the only demonstration of someone's having a conviction that his own life expresses it in action? Is not this the only guarantee that a person's so-called conviction is not changed every moment according to various things that happen to him and immediately change him and change everything for him, so that today he has faith and tomorrow has lost it and gains it again the day after tomorrow, until something very unusual happens so that he loses it almost entirely, assuming that he had it in the first place! (UDVS 69/SKS 8:177)

Not only does doubt become recognizable when one's words and actions do not correspond, but any further use of language, particularly the production of reasons, may exacerbate doubt.

> The demonstration of Christianity really lies in *imitation*. This was taken away. Then the need for 'reasons' was felt, but these reasons, or that there are reasons, are already a kind of doubt—and thus doubt arose and lived on reasons. It was not observed that the more reasons one advances, the more one nourishes doubt and the stronger it becomes, that offering doubt reasons in order to kill it is just like offering the tasty food it likes best of all to a hungry monster one wishes to eliminate. (FSE 68/SKS 13:91)

The imitation of Christ calls for a "decisive act" based in silence. Distraction and reason-seeking doubt must first be cleared away so that silence can be the "fundamental tone" (FSE 49/SKS 13:75). Only then, may one strive to replicate "the silent and veracious eloquence" of Christ's actions. Silence, therefore, describes both the setting for the imitation of Christ (one that is devoid of the noise of distraction) and the actual performance of the imitation of Christ where the emphasis is placed on doing, rather than saying. Kierkegaard writes that Christ's life was "an examination in obedience" that "he passed . . . at every moment until his death" (PC 183/SKS 12:183). Imitation means to follow Christ's example of obedient action; "unconditional obedience would not be to say a word about it but to act" (JP 1:299/Pap. VIII-2 B 88). The imitation of Christ involves silence in two main ways: 1) affirming the truth of inwardness, and 2) communication through action.

SILENCE AND THE IMPERATIVE TO LOVE

The second imperative of the second ethics is to love the neighbor. In *Works of Love*, Kierkegaard writes that this imperative depends on a very specific meaning of love, namely Christian love (*Kjerlighed*), which is distinguished from indirect forms of self-love such as erotic love and friendship. Since "it is Christianity's intention to wrest self-love away from us humanbeings" (WL 17/SKS 9:26), the imperative to love the neighbor "as with a pick, wrenches open the lock of self-love and wrests it away from a person" (WL 17/SKS 9:26). Christianity presupposes the ease and allure of self-love in contrast to the difficulty of extending love to others without a promise of reciprocation or reward. Therefore, Christian love is set forth as a *task* whose beneficiary is "the neighbor" who is not the specific lover, friend, enemy, nor stranger, but rather is representative of all people, irrespective of their relation to the self. "It is in fact Christian love that discovers and knows that the neighbor exists and, what is the same thing, that everyone is the neighbor. If it were not a duty to love, the concept 'neighbor' would not exist either; but only when one loves the neighbor, only then is the selfishness in preferential love rooted out and the equality of the eternal preserved" (WL 44/SKS 9:51). Kierkegaard identifies Christian love's two-fold activity: 1) it works in opposition to the "selfishness in preferential love," and 2) it works in favor of "equality." Silence aids both of these activities.

Kierkegaard considers all love, with the exception of Christian love, to be forms of preferential love, and therefore also self-love. These forms of love, of which he specifically mentions erotic love and friendship, are characterized by exclusivity, selectivity, and natural inclination.

> . . . erotic love and friendship are the very peak of self-esteem, the *I* intoxicated in the *other I*. The more securely one *I* and another *I* join to become one *I*, the more this united *I* selfishly cuts itself off from everyone else. At the peak of erotic love and friendship, the two actually do become one self, one *I*. This is explainable only because in preferential love there is a natural determinant (drive, inclination) and self-love, which selfishly can unite the two in a new selfish self. (WL 56/SKS 9:64)

Preferential love focuses attention only on a specific, self-concerned *I*. Kierkegaard calls worldly self-concern "sagacity;" "Acting sagaciously is . . . whereby one undeniably gets furthest ahead in the world, wins the world's goods and advantages and the world's honor" (WL 261/SKS 9:260). Sagacity refers to the activity of selecting and seeking out one's own preferences in order to gain advantage. Therefore, silence is sagacious if it is purposeful concealment intended to give the self some sort of advantage.[3] There are parallels between sagacious silence and deceitful silence mentioned in Chapter 1, in which silence is part of a "careful strategy" (Taylor 1981, 172). One way in which sagacious silence can be put into use is to conceal "unfavorable circumstances:"

> In temporality, when the task is to be sagacious to one's own advantage, when worldly sagacity judges and evaluates, then unfavorable circumstances are not merely a defense for silence, but silence is admired as sagacity, whereas favorable circumstances are an invitation for all to put in a word . . . remaining silent is not like sleeping, in the sense that the one who is sleeping does not sin, inasmuch as the single individual has incurred shocking guilt in the world—by remaining silent. The guilt was not that he did not get the circumstances changed; the guilt was that he remained silent, not out of sober-mindedness that remains silent when it is proper to remain silent, but out of sagacity that is silent because it is the most sagacious. (UDVS 150/SKS 8:246–7)

Sagacity is counter-productive to the duty of Christian love which disregards preference. According to Kierkegaard, sagacious silence is ethically reprehensible and incurs guilt because it is motivated by an excessive concern for self and a regard for the world's judgment, rather than being motivated by a concern for the neighbor and a regard for the eternal's judgment.

> Acting sagaciously is, actually, a *halfway approach*, whereby one undeniably gets furthest ahead in the world, wins the world's goods and advantages and the world's honor, because, in the eternal sense, the world and the world's advantages are half-measures. But neither the eternal nor Holy Scripture has taught anyone to aspire to get ahead or furthest ahead in the world; on the contrary, it warns against getting too far ahead in the world in order, if possible, to keep oneself unstained by the defilement of the world. But if this is so, then aspiring to get ahead or furthest ahead in the world does not seem commendable. (WL 261/SKS 9:260)

Although silence may serve sagacity, the opposite is also true; silence can thwart sagacity. Just as silence can hide one's own weaknesses, as is in the case with sagacious silence, silence can also hide one strengths. Humility can also, then, involve a purposeful concealment. However, humility and sagacity are differentiated by *what* they hide; humility conceals that which sagacity advises to broadcast, and sagacity conceals that which humility leaves unhidden. Sagacious silence and humble silence are the inverse of each other; "In situations where my silence will make me seem worse than I am, I should be silent—for instance, giving alms in secret. Where my silence will make me seem better than I am, then I should speak—confession of sin. The good a man does he should, if possible, keep to himself, the evil he has done he should speak about" (JP 4:99/SKS 22:246). This formula for behavior is ill-advised by the standard of sagacity. Sagacity sanctions self-promotion and boastfulness. Currently, sagacity finds a perfect vehicle in social media where over-sharing and constant curation of one's online image are normalized.

Christian love, on the other hand, encourages self-denial and humility; "Wherever the essentially Christian is, there is also self-denial, which is Christianity's essential form"(WL 56/SKS 9:64). Bragging about oneself is not an act of love; "The one who loves humbles himself before the good . . . the one who loves hides himself" (WL 340/SKS 9:334–5). Christian love seeks to shift the focus away from the specific, self-concerned *I*, and thereby make possible the extension of one's concern beyond the self. Silence, as an expression of self-denial and humility, is ultimately an expression of love for the neighbor since it halts the absorbing and exclusive activity of preferential love.

Kierkegaard maintains that in order for one's actions of self-denial and humility to count, those actions cannot be motivated by a hidden sagacity of wanting be judged favorably by others because of them.[4] But the discernment of someone's motivation is difficult because it is invisible from the outside, even if a motivation leads to outward actions; ". . . self-denial is required *inwardly* and self-sacrificing unselfishness *outwardly*. If, then, someone . . . is asked whether it is actually out of love on his part that he does it, the answer must be: 'No one else can decide this for certain; it is possible that it is vanity, pride—in short, something bad, but it is also possible that it is love" (WL 374/SKS 9:367). Furthermore, even sincere attempts at self-knowledge may not fully reveal one's motivations to oneself.

Christian love's movement away from the self's preferences is simultaneously an extension of concern toward the neighbor. This new object of concern is, by its very definition, one's equal: "The neighbor is the one who is equal" (WL 60/SKS 9:67). While preferential love is determined by people's dissimilarities,[5] Christian love commands equality in love that mirrors humanity's "eternal equality before God" (WL 68/SKS 9:75).

> Love for the neighbor is therefore the eternal equality in loving, but the eternal equality is the opposite of preference. This needs no elaborate development. Equality is simply not to make distinctions, and eternal equality is unconditionally not to make the slightest distinction, unqualifiedly not to make the

slightest distinction. Preference, on the other hand, is to make distinctions; passionate preference is unqualifiedly to make distinctions. (WL 58/SKS 9:65)

Genuine Christian love equalizes. In *Upbuilding Discourses in Various Spirits* and *Works of Love*, Kierkegaard gives two specific examples of silence that perform the function of equalizing: 1) silence can diminish the natural activity of comparison, and 2) silence can hide the neighbor's sin.

In Part II of *Upbuilding Discourses in Various Spirits* titled "What We Learn from the Lilies in the Field and from the Birds of the Air," Kierkegaard begins by discussing worry and the lesson to be learned from the lilies and the birds concerning "To Be Contented With Being A Human Being." Kierkegaard illustrates the lesson by means of a parable about a lily, who in comparing itself to more beautiful and better situated lilies became worried, "preoccupied with itself and the condition of its life—all the day long" (UDVS 168/SKS 8:268). The parable is, of course, allegorical since "the lily is the human being" (UDVS 169/SKS 8:268). Kierkegaard believes that worry is derived from comparison. "All worldly worry has its basis in a person's unwillingness to be contented with being a human being, in his worried craving for distinction by way of comparison" (UDVS 171/SKS 8:270). The parable's purpose is to show the corruption of comparison and how it induces worry by "putting the human being in someone else's place or putting someone else in his place" (UDVS 169/SKS 8:268). While to speak of one's "place" in order to judge its superiority or inferiority in relation to someone else's "place" may be sagacious, it is also antithetical to the aim of Christian love. The lilies and the birds exemplify the equality of Christian love by their liberation from comparison and worry, precisely because they cannot speak. The lesson they teach is succinctly stated in another of Kierkegaard's books that discusses the same topic: "From the lily and the bird as teachers, let us learn *silence*, or learn to *be silent*" (WA 10/SKS 11:16).

Kierkegaard claims the conditions for comparison are inescapable when two people are present to each other. "No individual can be present, even though in silence, in such a way that his presence means nothing at all by way of comparison" (UDVS 161/SKS 8:262). Such comparison is unavoidable in conversation.

> All misapprehension, after all, stems from speech, more specifically from a comparison that is implicit in talking, especially in conversation. For example, when the happy person says to one who is worried: Be glad, the remark also implies: as I am glad; and when the strong person says: Be strong, it is tacitly understood, as I am strong. (UDVS 160–61/SKS 8:261)

Although silence cannot remove the possibility of comparison, which inevitably exists when two people are together, silence can diminish comparison through the simple act of halting conversation. By halting conversation, Job's friends, for example, minimized the comparison between their own situations and Job's suffering; "But silence respects the worry and respects the worried one as Job's friends did, who out of respect sat silent with the sufferer and held him in respect" (UDVS 161/SKS 8:262). Comparison only ceases altogether in pure silence that exists when one is alone, or the equivalent, which, according to Kierkegaard, is being in nature or with children.[6] Therefore, choosing to be silent in the presence of someone else can be, in a sense, an attempt to make oneself invisible to the other in order to reduce comparison. Kierkegaard offers this possibility through the example of a teacher and pupil:

> The one who truly loves, who could not find it in his heart at any price to let the beloved girl feel his superiority, communicates the truth to her in such a way that she does not notice that he is the teacher, he lures it out of her, places it upon her lips, and thus hears not himself say it but her, or he helps the truth forward and hides himself. (WL 341/SKS 9:336)[7]

Silence produced out of "solicitude" and "respect" for the other is yet another form of purposeful concealment of the self. Yet this concealment does not merely subordinate the assumed preference of the self to speak and sagaciously compare,[8] it also functions as an equalizer by not mentioning, and thereby deemphasizing, the distinctions between the self and the neighbor.

Another way in which silence contributes to the equality of the neighbor is by hiding the neighbor's sin. Of course, Kierkegaard is not advocating turning a blind eye to harms so that they are passively permitted nor is he endorsing complicity with the other's sin. Rather, Kierkegaard is saying that the neighbor's faults should not be highlighted in a way that subordinates the status of the neighbor in relation to the self. Love's connection to hiding sin has a Scriptural basis; Kierkegaard considers the text of 1 Peter 4:8: "Above all hold unfailing your love for one another, since love covers a multitude of sins." Kierkegaard considers the role silence has in this expression of love for the neighbor; "*Love hides a multitude of sins: what it cannot avoid seeing or hearing, it hides by silence*, by a *mitigating explanation*, by *forgiveness*. By *silence* it hides the multitude" (WL 289/SKS 9:286).[9]

According to Kierkegaard, love does not "discover sins" (WL 282/SKS 9:280). Instead, the one who loves "expresses the apostolic injunction to be a child in evil" (WL 285/SKS 9:284), and therefore lives in a certain state of innocence, of willful naivety in relation to the existence of other people's sin. In the times when the one who loves "cannot avoid seeing or hearing" the sins of others, they are not to ignore the sins, nor expose them to other people, but take the sins seriously and hide them.

> But this is the way the one who loves conducts himself when he as inadvertently, quite accidentally; never because he himself has sought an opportunity

for it, becomes aware of a person's sin, his fault, of what he has committed or how he has been carried away by a weakness—the loving one keeps silent about it and hides a multitude of sins. (WL 289/SKS 9:287)

Just as silence does not totally terminate comparison, silence also is not the most ideal response to the neighbor's sin. Kierkegaard writes that a "mitigating explanation" (WL 291/SKS 9:303) subtracts from the sin and that forgiveness removes sin:

> Keeping silence does not actually take away anything from the generally known multitude of sins. The mitigating explanation wrests something away from the multitude by showing that this and that were not sin. Forgiveness removes what cannot be denied to be sin. Thus love strives in every way to hide a multitude of sins; but forgiveness is the most notable way. (WL 294/SKS 9:291)

Although silence does not subtract from or remove the neighbor's sin, Kierkegaard nevertheless considers silence an appropriate response because it indicates a proper seriousness in relation to sin, and it does not increase the sin. Silence combats one's natural "inclination to see his neighbor's faults" and his "even greater one to want to tell them" (WL 290/SKS 9:287). The alternative to silence, chatter (*snakke*), not only reflects "light-minded[ness]" (WL 289/SKS 9:287) in relation to the neighbor's sin, but it also incurs "guilt" (WL 289/SKS 9:287). "The neighbor's fault is and ought to be too serious a matter; therefore to chatter inquisitively, frivolously, and enviously about it is a sign of corruption. But the one who by telling the neighbor's faults helps to corrupt people is of course increasing the multitude of sins" (WL 290/SKS 9:287).

Silence concerning the neighbor's sin contributes to the equality of the neighbor. Rather than using the neighbor's weakness as an object for an "entertaining story" to "momentarily . . . obtain an attentive audience" (WL 290/SKS 9:287), the one who loves regards the neighbor and their sin in all seriousness by remaining silent. Within the second ethics, the imperative to love confers ethical value on a consideration of who will receive benefit from particular statements and actions. When the neighbor does not benefit from a particular statement or action, as in the case of revealing the neighbor's sin, the imperative to love overrules the first ethics' demand for complete disclosure. Kierkegaard contends that the power of self-love is so great that it must be counteracted by the surrender of one's own personal benefit for the benefit of the neighbor. This surrender may entail the humble concealment of the self's strengths, as well as the merciful concealment of the neighbor's weaknesses. Silence, as the means of this purposeful concealment, takes away benefit from the self and gives it to the neighbor and thereby equalizes the self and neighbor through Christian love.

In summary, the silence operates to fulfill the imperatives of the second ethics. The imitation of Christ requires silence for affirming the truth of inwardness and in communicating through action. Love for the neighbor requires silence to oppose preference and endorse equality, by bringing down the status of the self and bringing up the status of the neighbor.

NOTES

1. It is interesting to note that Kierkegaard's concern with misunderstanding lasted through the later stages of his authorship. Near the end of his life, it appears that at least to some degree, he gave up on indirect communication because it posed barriers between the content of his writings and his readers. See, for example, "Meanwhile I came by way of further reflection to the realization that it perhaps is more appropriate for me to make at least an attempt once again to use my pen but in a different way, as I would use my voice, consequently in direct address to my contemporaries, winning men, if possible" (FSE ix/Pap. X-6 B 4:3).

2. My emphasis.

3. Language is similar to silence in this regard. Kierkegaard writes that language may also be used for purposeful concealment: ". . . one person can hide much from another by remaining silent, at times even more by speaking" (UDVS 22/SKS 8:137).

4. See, for example, "A person makes Christian humility and self-denial empty when he indeed denies himself in one respect but does not have the courage to do it decisively, and therefore he takes care to be understood in his humility and his self-denial; and then he becomes honored and esteemed for his humility and self-denial—which certainly is not self-denial" (WL 374/SKS 9:367).

5. Kierkegaard states that dissimilarity inspires preferential love. The subjects of preferential love unite in such a way that they are separated from all others in their love, and are set apart:

> In erotic love and friendship, the two love each other by virtue of the dissimilarity or by virtue of the similarity that is based in dissimilarity (as when two friends love each other by virtue of similar customs, characters, occupations, education, etc,. that is, on the basis of the similarity by which they are different from other people, or in which they are like each other as different from other people. (WL 56/SKS 9:61)

6. Kierkegaard writes that when one is in nature or with children, one is in the silence of aloneness. See, for example: ". . . out where the lily blooms so beautifully, in the field, up there where the bird is freely at home, in the heavens, if comfort is being sought—there is unbroken silence; no one is present there, and everything is sheer persuasion" (UDVS 161/SKS 8:262), and "How often has not a sufferer experienced and movingly sensed that when only a child is present there is still no one present" (UDVS 161/SKS 8:262).

7. This recalls the discussion of the maieutic method in Chapter 3.

8. Kierkegaard writes that in many instances, the self prefers speaking over silence, particularly when it is sagacious and therefore unethical. In *Without Authority*, he writes that speaking "tempts:" "But because the ability to speak is an advantage, it does not follow that the ability to be silent would not be an art or would be an inferior art. On the contrary, because the human being is able to speak, the ability to be silent is an art, and a great art precisely because this advantage of his so easily tempts him" (WA 10/SKS 11:18).

9. In this passage, Kierkegaard does not use the Danish word *Tavshed* to indicate silence (as he does in the *Upbuilding Discourses in Various Spirits* passage discussed in the preceding section). Kierkegaard writes, "*Kjerlighed skjuler Syndernes Mangfoldighed; thi hvad den ikke kan undgaa at see eller høre, det skjuler den ved Fortielse, ved formildende Forklaring, ved Tilgivelse. Ved Fortielse skjuler den Mangfoldigheden*" (SKS 9:286). However, Kierkegaard's

use of *Fortielse* preserves the sense of silence that is relevant here: concealment, secrecy, not saying something that can be said.

Chapter Six

Exemplars of Communication

Here lies a problem: if there is a tendency to misuse language and furthermore, if language cannot even essentially communicate what is most important for Kierkegaard, namely ethical and religious content, then how is it to be communicated, if at all? Kierkegaard employed a panoply of literary devices to pose this problem, and then pointed to Socrates and non-human life as paradigms for effective communication. In chapter 3, double-reflection and reduplication were discussed as methods of communication. In a double-reflection, the communication is presented as a puzzle; Socrates and his declaration of ignorance is an example of this kind. In a reduplication, the communicator is the puzzle, as a living model of what is being communicated; non-human organisms can be an example of this kind. It will be recalled that for a "communication of knowledge" the object of the communication is given by the communicator to the receiver. In a "communication of capability" emphasis on the *object* of the communication is exchanged for emphasis on the *way* in which the communication is conducted. A communication of ethical or religious capability requires a double-reflection and/or reduplication. A "communication of knowledge" requires words, but a "communication of capability" as an instruction in a way of being, should, at least to some extent, exclude words. Kierkegaard wrote, "Herein lies the truth in Pythagorean instruction, to begin with silence. This was a way of gaining consciousness of the concrete" (JP 3:7/SKS 22:380).

SOCRATES

Socrates is a frequent motif in Kierkegaard's work, and he stands for not only an exemplar of a philosopher who lives in a way that is consistent with his philosophy, but he also is effective at using the communicative method of double-reflection. The most notable example of his use of this method is his profession of ignorance. After being charged with impiety and corruption of the youth, Socrates explains to the jury that he suffers from a poor reputation caused by a "certain kind of wisdom" (Plato 1997, 58). He gives the following proof for his wisdom:

> Do not create a disturbance, gentlemen, even if you think I am boasting, for the story I shall tell does not originate with me, but I will refer you to a trustworthy source. I shall call upon the god at Delphi as witness to the existence and nature of my wisdom, if it be such. You know Chaerephon. He was my friend from youth, and the friend of most of you, as he shared your exile and your return. You surely know the kind of man he was, how impulsive in any course of action. He went to Delphi at one time and ventured to ask the oracle—as I say, gentlemen, do not create a disturbance—he asked if any man was wiser than I, and the Pythian replied that no one was wiser. (Plato 1997, 58)

Socrates' initial response to and interpretation of the oracle's pronouncement is most unusual. Rather than feeling self-congratulatory that he is the wisest, Socrates claims to be puzzled by this "riddle" and then "proceed[s] systematically" to examine his fellow Athenians to see whether it was true. At the end these examinations, Socrates concludes that he is, in fact, the wisest. But this conclusion contains a double paradox. The first paradox consists in the equation of wisdom with the acknowledgement of ignorance. Socrates' wisdom exceeds that of his fellow citizens because they cannot tell the difference between what they know and what they do not know. He said he differed from his fellow Athenian, ". . . he thinks he knows something when he does not, whereas when I do not know, neither do I think I know; so I am likely to be wiser than he to this small extent, that I do not think I know what I do not know" (Plato 1997, 59). Even his initial response before arriving at this conclusion—specifically, his puzzlement and subsequent inquiry—already showcases Socrates' ignorance; he is the wisest, but he does not know he is wisest. The second paradox consists in the equation of value and worthlessness. On the one hand, there is value in obtaining wisdom (after all, isn't this the aim of philosophy and the ground of Socrates' authority?), and on the other hand, Socrates undermines this value by claiming that human wisdom is valueless. Socrates interprets the oracle's claim of his wisdom to mean "This man among you, mortals, is wisest who, like Socrates, understands that his wisdom is worthless" (Plato 1997, 60).

In 1759, Johann Georg Hamann wrote *Socratic Memorabilia*, in which the second section contains an extended discussion of Socratic ignorance. In 1844, Kierkegaard wrote in his journals that "[Hamann] has said the best that has been said about Socrates" (JP 2:204/Pap. V B 45). Hamann was an early and powerful influence on Kierkegaard's interpretation of Socrates, and more specifically on his understanding of Socratic ignorance. Hamann is mentioned repeatedly in Kierkegaard's journals between 1836 and 1850, and Kierkegaard also notes a specific Hamann reading period[1] prior to his own dissertation on Socrates in 1841. Although Kierkegaard's views on Socrates certainly evolve throughout his authorship, it is easy to trace Hamann's inspiration for Kierkegaard's thinking in the period prior to his dissertation through his publication of *The Concept of Anxiety* in 1844, a work that is bracketed by an epigraph about Hamann and Socratic ignorance and a concluding footnote referring to Hamann's *Socratic Memorabilia*.

Hamann's *Socratic Memorabilia* is dedicated "to the two:" Hamann's friend, Christoph Berens, and Berens's friend, Immanuel Kant, who deemed it their mission to convince Hamann to rejoin the cause of the Enlightenment after his religious revelation and conversion. This text, Hamann's response to Berens and Kant, relies on the example of Socrates as the philosophical paradigm to critique their attempt to reconvert Hamann to the fundamentally humanist Enlightenment project. As Socrates opposed the sophists who claimed to know more than they did, Hamann also opposed the Enlightenment thinkers who claimed to know more than they did.[2] Hamann wrote that Socrates' profession of ignorance distanced him from those who touted their possession of knowledge and their sycophants, and brought him closer to his students by identifying with them in their state of not knowing.[3]

But this aspect of the claim of ignorance is therefore a form of deception or purposeful concealment, intended to be to "a certain extent an insult" (Hamann 1967, 161). This insult is described through Hamann's analogy of two kinds of card players. One player says "I don't play" which means that either he doesn't "understand the game or that he [has] an aversion to it" (Hamann 1967, 165). The other player, in contrast, is "an honorable man, who [is] known to possess every possible skill in the game, and who [is] well versed in its rules and in its forbidden tricks" (Hamann 1967, 165). If this player were to say "I don't play," Hamann writes, his meaning would be different than that of the first player; instead it would be a refusal to play with "clever swindlers." Hamann writes,

> ... we would have to join him [that is, the skilled player] in looking the people with whom he was talking straight in the face, and would be able to supplement his words as follows: 'I don't play,' that is, with people such as you, who break the rules of the game, and rob it of its pleasure. If you offer to play a game, our mutual agreement, then, is that we recognize the capriciousness of chance as our master; and you call the science of your nimble fingers chance, and I must accept it as such, if I will, or run the risk of insulting you or choose the shame of imitating you. If you had proposed to me that we hold a contest to determine which one of us was the best slight-of-hand artist at cards, then I would have wanted to answer differently, and perhaps to join in a game in

order to show you that you have learned to fix cards as poorly as you understand how to play those that are dealt to you according to the rules of the game. The opinion of Socrates can be summed in these blunt words, when he said to the Sophists, the learned men of his time, 'I know nothing.' Therefore these words were a thorn in their eyes and a scourge on their backs. (Hamann 1967, 165–67)

Hamann compares Socrates' claim of ignorance to the proficient card player who refuses to play a cheapened version of the game, one that mocks the sincere purpose of the game by focusing on winning and showing off in front of others. The result is that the humility of the master philosopher/card player shames the hubris of the lesser philosophers and "clever swindlers." The response of "I don't play" is the same kind of response as Socrates' "I don't know" in that they conceal or are *silent* about true meanings. The other cards players are meant to figure out that "I do not play" means "I do not play because we do not share purposes." The contemporaries of Socrates are meant to figure out that "I do not know" means "I know my knowledge has limits and that my knowledge doesn't compare to what the gods know." In her commentary on *Socratic Memorabilia*, Gwen Griffith-Dickson (1995, 47) wrote that Hamann used the example of card playing purposely to represent Socrates' "rejection of the lust for knowledge which possessed the Athenians, the Sophists; it was his refusal to join in this vice." In this way, the master card player and Socrates present a "double-reflection," an indirect communication that presents a puzzle for others to solve for themselves as a form of ethical education.

Furthermore, Socrates' role as a philosophical paradigm is significant because Hamann knew that Kant revered Socrates. Frederick Beiser (1987, 26) points out in his book, *The Fate of Reason*, that Hamann invokes Socrates, the "favorite patron saint" of the Enlightenment philosophers, against the Enlightenment philosophers themselves by deploying a new interpretation of him as "the pagan apostle of faith against the tyranny of reason" (Beiser 1987, 26). More specifically, by using Socrates as an example of humility, Hamann implicates Kant as a Sophist who didn't truly understand the master. This misunderstanding is so profound that Kant (1929, 30), for example in the *Critique of Pure Reason*, highlights Socrates' skill in revealing the ignorance in his opponents while remaining silent on Socrates' revelation of his own ignorance: ". . . Socratic fashion, namely, by the clearest proof of the ignorance of the objectors."

For Kierkegaard, the relationships between Socrates and the Sophists, Hamann and Enlightenment proponents (represented by Kant and Berens), as well as the basic misunderstandings exposed by these relationships, produce humor. He writes,

> The ignorance of the Xn [Christian] (this purely Socratic view, as, e.g. in a Hamann) is, of course also humorous, for what does it amount to other than this forcing oneself down to the lowest position and looking up (i.e., down) at the common view, yet in such a way that behind this self-degradation lies a high degree of self-elevation (the humility of the Xn [Christian], e.g., what in its polemical form against the world makes profession of its own wretchedness, which on the other hand, in its normal form, it involves a noble pride . . .) (KJN 1:208–210/SKS 17:216)

Particularly in his journals from 1837, Kierkegaard used Socrates and Hamann to work through the concepts of irony and humor. In June of that year, Kierkegaard identifies Socrates and Hamann as archetypes of humor. However, in July, Kierkegaard wrote that Socrates' position is that of irony, while Hamann ascends to the humorous because of his Christianity. Kierkegaard writes,

> Irony can no doubt also produce a certain calm (which may then correspond to the peace that follows a humorous development), which, however, is a long way from being Christian reconciliation. . . . It can produce a certain love, the kind with which e.g. Socrates encompassed his disciples (spiritual pederasty, as Hamann says), but it is still egoistic, because he stood as their deliverer, expanded their anxious expressions and views in his higher consciousness, in this point of view . . . (KJN 1:216/SKS 17:225)

The paradox presented by the unity of wisdom and ignorance functions to offend, insult, and humiliate those who avow comprehensive knowledge. The second paradox presented by the unity of wisdom's worth and worthlessness, on the other hand, is not truly a paradox, but rather emerges from a confusion between human wisdom and divine wisdom. Whereas the sophist and advocates of the Enlightenment scurry to achieve human wisdom in its various forms of empirical knowledge and rhetorical and philosophical skill, Hamann and Kierkegaard interpret Socratic ignorance as distinguishing between the ultimate worthlessness of human wisdom (as worthless in the long run as playing a game of cards, as in Hamann's analogy) and the ultimate worth of divine wisdom. This is why it is important to note that Socrates' wisdom is not given on his own authority, but the authority of the divine oracle and the Socratic daemon. As with the first paradox, this aspect of Socratic ignorance is also offensive because it requires the submission of reason to the divine. Hamann, well acquainted with his philosophical contemporaries, wrote, "The transmission of a divine oracle means, however, as little as the appearance of a comet for a philosopher of modern taste" (Hamann 1967, 157). Socratic ignorance therefore illuminates the cross-purposes of Hamann's and Kant's projects. In his excellent book on Hamann, John Betz (2008, 79) writes,

> For the *Aufklärer* the purpose of reason is to question the authority of tradition in the name of free inquiry, thereby de facto replacing the authority of tradition with that of the autonomous individual, regardless of his or her moral formation. For Hamann, on the other hand, the purpose of reason is precisely to deconstruct all proud knowledge falsely so called, the kind of knowledge which is really *doxa* but nevertheless opposes itself to faith, so that true knowledge can begin: the kind of knowledge that is born of humility and leads to love. . . . Indeed, for Hamann it is only through a suffering of reason's limitations that philosophy properly begins, having been prepared by a kind of *docta ignorantia* for the light of faith. . . .

For the Sophists and Enlightenment advocates, reason's end is itself; for Socrates and Hamann, reason is traversed to its limit and the final end is transcendent. Reason's limit cannot properly be seen, however, when our conception of it is bloated and its boundary is denied or obscured. Hamann writes,

> In this connection Socrates therefore imitated his father, a sculptor, who, by removing and cutting away what should not be in the wood, precisely in so doing, furthers the form of the image. Therefore, the great men of his time had sufficient reason to cry out against him that he was cutting down all the oaks of their forests, spoiling all of their logs, and that he only knew how to make chips out of their wood. (Hamann 1967, 153)

Socratic ignorance is not simply a negative endeavor of cutting away and revealing falsehoods, but rather is positive in the sense that it clears away the ground for the construction of genuine self-knowledge. The imperative, "Know Thyself," posted over the door of the temple at Delphi, requires destruction then construction. Hamann uses the images of birth and death: "the grain of all our natural wisdom must decay, must perish in ignorance, and . . . the life and being of a higher knowledge must spring forth newly created from this death, from this nothing" (Hamann 1967, 169). Kierkegaard and Hamann imbue this imperative with theological significance, since for them, self-knowledge means coming to grips with ourselves as other-created, rather than self-created. We are "homesick" for this understanding of ourselves, according to Kierkegaard and Hamann, and anxiety, "impertinent disquiet" (CA 162/SKS 4:460), and "holy hypochondria" (CA 162/SKS 4:460) are symptoms of our homesickness.

Additionally, self-knowledge is not something one comes to possess as an object of the intellect, but is something that requires the commitment of one's whole being. Hamann described this as "sensibility" (*Empfindung*), a word which means "not only . . . 'feeling' but also 'perception' . . . and thus carries connotations of receptive awareness and response, with a strongly physical undertone" (Griffith-Dickson 1995, 48). The difference between full-bodied being and abstract reasoning, a distinction effectively appropriated by

Kierkegaard, is intensely Hamannian. He sharply contrasts "sensibility" from "a theoretical proposition" (Hamann 1967, 167); a contrast he says holds "a greater difference than between a living animal and its anatomical skeleton" (Hamann 1967, 167). Those who treat Socratic ignorance as theoretical proposition rather than a sensibility again show a deep misunderstanding about what it means by putting it on as a sort of costume or disguise, they "wrap themselves . . . in the lion skin of Socratic ignorance" (Hamann 1967, 167). He calls this out as hypocrisy; he writes, "If they know nothing, why does the world need a learned demonstration of it? Their hypocrisy is ridiculous and insolent. Whoever needs so much acumen and eloquence to convince himself of his ignorance, however, must cherish in his heart a powerful repugnance for the truth of it" (Hamann 1967, 167).

Kierkegaard closely follows Hamann on this point: Socratic ignorance, as a form of self-knowledge, is an entire way of being. For example, this is clear in the epigraph for *The Concept of Anxiety*: ". . . Socrates still is what he was, the simple wise man, because of the peculiar distinction that he expressed both in words and life, something that the eccentric Hamann first reiterated with great admiration two thousand years later: 'For Socrates was great in 'that he distinguished between what he understood and what he did not understand'" (CA 3/SKS 4:310).

Socrates' ignorance was not merely a "theoretical proposition" nor the "anatomical skeleton" of the "living animal," but rather was "expressed both in words *and life*." I don't believe it is over-exaggeration to trace the existential emphasis on action from Kierkegaard, through Hamann, all the way back to Socrates.

These two meanings of Socratic ignorance, a tool to prompt humility and a sensibility one expresses through one's life, allow for a richer interpretation which defuses the debate about whether Socrates really meant his statements of ignorance. Socrates is wise in comparison with other men, yet Socrates is ignorant in comparison with the gods. So, as the expert card player says "I don't play" in order to refuse a game with those who aren't playing for the same purpose, Socrates says "I am ignorant" in order to refuse a game of philosophy with those who aren't playing philosophy for the same purpose. He thereby presents them with their own riddle, or double-reflection, concerning their wisdom, a riddle intended to lead them to the dictum over the temple door. *And* Socrates' confession of ignorance is also sincere; he defers to the authority of his daemon and the oracle who says "This man among you, mortals, is wisest who, like Socrates, understands that his wisdom is worthless" (Plato 1997, 60).

Chapter 6

NON-HUMAN LIFE

> So pay attention to the lily and the bird! Surely there is spirit in nature—especially when the Gospel inspires it, because then nature is pure symbol and pure instruction for man; it, too, is inspired by God and is 'profitable for instruction, for reproof, for correction.' (FSE 182/SKS 16:230)

Kierkegaard did not write extensively on nature, and it would be a stretch to say he had a philosophy of nature. However, Kierkegaard develops his critique of language and his theme of the problem of communication by discussing nature. More specifically, Kierkegaard considers how ethical and religious communication can be expressed through non-human organisms[4] such as lilies, birds, and animals. The communicative value of these organisms depends precisely on their inability to use human language and therefore they necessarily avoid the misuse of language. Furthermore, by avoiding these failures, nature provides a vivid "symbol" for "instruction" by showing how sharply nature's communication contrasts with human language.

Language is often touted as humanity's great distinguishing feature[5] that gives us a privileged status among animals, but Kierkegaard questions this firmly embedded and value-laden assumption by pointing to examples in nature that communicate more effectively than through language. It is precisely the silence of nature, its wordlessness, that elevates its communicative ability over language because in silence it embodies that which it communicates. Rather than talking about how to live without anxiety, the lilies and birds, favorite examples used by Kierkegaard,[6] show it through their existence. Without language, animals cannot provide public explanations for their behavior separate from what their actions explicitly express. Without language, animals cannot say they are something other than what they are.

> Animal life is so simple, so easy to understand, because the animal has the advantage over man of not being able to talk. The only talking in animal existence is its life, its actions.
>
> When, for example, I see a deer in heat, I see what it means, that the deer is in the grip of a powerful drive, and there is nothing further to say about it. If it could talk, we would perhaps hear some rubbish about its being motivated by a sense of duty, that out of duty to society and the race it wants to propagate the species, plus the fact that it is performing the greatest service etc.
>
> When I see a spider spinning its fine web, truly a work of art, I see—for the spider has the advantage over man of not being able to talk—I see what it means, the spider is seeking a living. If the spider could talk, I would probably hear—while it sits hungrily watching the web to see if a fly would come—a long discussion about its enthusiasm for art which lay behind the production of this fine web, which actually is a work of art.
>
> And so it is everywhere in the animal world.

> Take the power of speech from man—and you will see that human existence will no longer be so difficult to explain.
> The thing that confuses everything is this advantage man has over the animal, his ability to talk. It permits a person's life to express the lowest while his mouth prattles about the highest and *to give assurances* that this is what determines him. (JP 3:13–14/SKS 26:392)

The deer in heat and the spider spinning its web can only express what they really are: moved by hunger for sex or food. Kierkegaard imagines what the deer and spider could say if they could use language. Instead of seeking sex and food, the most basic of living drives, they could describe the motivations for their actions in other terms, such as fulfilling a duty "to propagate the species" or artistic "enthusiasm." In this imaginative moment, the deer and spider are transformed into humans whose mouths prattle "about the highest." When Kierkegaard imagines the speaking deer and spider, we recognize ourselves, silly and pathetic creatures who use words to rationalize our behavior as something higher or more flattering than what it really is. This passage functions as a fable in which speaking animals provide an instructive lesson for humans.

The exchange of the true action for the untrue rationalization put to words is the risk posed by the use of language. It's not necessary that this exchange always happens when language is used, but Kierkegaard wishes to alert his reader to the burden involved with having the capacity to use language.

> Language, the gift of speech, engulfs the human race in such a cloud of drivel and twaddle that it becomes its ruination. God alone knows how many there are in every generation who have not been ruined by talking, who have not been transformed to prattlers or hypocrites. Only the most outstanding personalities of the human race are able to bear this advantage, the power of speech. So dubious is this advantage which man has over the animal, an advantage which often, ironically, means that he is what the deer is not: a babbler or a hypocrite. (JP 3:14/SKS 26:392)

"[T]he power of speech" as an "advantage" we possess yet also must "bear," can lead to our ruin when we are overconfident in its abilities to express everything and misuse it. We can be "ruined by talking."

Kierkegaard directs his reader to observe nature as a correct and living model for communication through action and being. But what is it, exactly, that nature communicates? What meanings are to be found in nature? What is the "object" of nature's communication? For Kierkegaard, nature has no message of its own, and it would be a mistake to think it does.[7] Rather the "symbol" and "instruction for man" (FSE 182/SKS 16:230) of nature is created by God[8] and interpreted by human thought. Within the Lutheran tradition, nature is where we see the "masks" of God and "where the hidden God is revealed" (Rasmussen 1996, 279).[9] Nature itself is indifferent to meaning. Therefore, a communication by nature that is indifferent to meaning requires that the receiver of the communication comes up with the meaning himself. This is different from irony in which "words . . . express something other than . . . [their] literal meaning" (Webster's), because there are no words and no literal meaning; the communication simply expresses "something other." The "something other" is what you, as the receiver, are to work out "by yourself for yourself" (Vlastos 1992, 79). Nature's communication does not rely on irony, but is another form of indirect communication that also "acknowledg[es] the burden of freedom which is inherent in all significant communication" (Vlastos 1992, 79). By reflecting on nature's communication, one becomes a listener, observer, and interpreter, rather than "a babbler or a hypocrite" (JP 3:14/SKS 26:392). But note that in the act of interpreting, however, we return to our language by producing and grasping meanings. The consequence of all of this is not to discard language and idolize nature,[10] but rather to draw attention to Kierkegaard's corrective, one which continues to be relevant: we are responsible for the possible and careless misuse of language and should acknowledge that language's power is limited—we cannot say everything. Kierkegaard directs us to consider the "eloquence of silence" (PC 14/SKS 12:24) in nature and to use this as a starting point for essential speaking and attendance to our serious tasks and choices.

NOTES

1. Kierkegaard: "from the time I was reading Hamann" (Pap. IX B 33:3).
2. Betz (2008, 76) writes, "Socrates continues to be a mask for Hamann himself in his dealings with Kant and Berens."
3. Hamann (1967, 165) writes,

> If Socrates rendered an accounting to Crito with his statement: 'I know nothing,' if he turned away, with precisely this dictum, the learned and curious Athenians, and, while seeking to make it easier for his handsome youths to renounce their vanity, he sought to gain their confidence through his equality with them, then the restatements of his motto which one would have to make according to this threefold point of view would appear as different as three brothers who are sons of the same father sometimes do.

4. It appears that Kierkegaard thought that non-living nature (e.g. clouds, autumnal weather, etc. . . .) communicates nothing except for the aesthetic meanings we provide. Some examples include: "Sometimes when the whole sky is overcast, one see a little strip, a little patch, which seems to dream of a bliss of its own and to radiate a glory from within itself" (JP 3:256/SKS 18:46), and "Autumn is: the time of longings, the time of colors, the time of cloud, the time of sounds (sound is transmitted far more animatedly and swiftly than in the oppressive summer heat), the time of recollections" (JP 3:259/Pap. VII-1 B 205).
5. "It is all well enough that 'language' distinguishes man from the animal. . ." (JP 3:7/SKS 22:380)

6. The lilies and the birds are a focal point for earlier scholarship about Kierkegaard's views concerning silence, specifically religious silence. See, for example, Wanda Warren Berry's "The Silent Woman in Kierkegaard's Later Religious Writings" (1997).

7. Kierkegaard writes that Adler is guilty of this mistake: "Adler's dizziness is apparent also in his careless, loose thinking and believing that greatness will prevail even if wrong and injustice also occur, and the best proof of this dizziness is his constant appeal to analogies from nature, for nature simply is not the ethical; nature allows rain to fall on good and evil alike, but the ethical makes the qualitative distinction. . ." (JP 3:263/Pap. VII-2 B 256).

8. "Surely there is spirit in nature—especially when *the Gospel inspirits it*, because then nature is pure symbol and pure instruction for man; it, too, is *inspired by God*. . ." (FSE 182/ SKS 16:230) [My emphasis].

9. In *Earth Community/Earth Ethics*, Larry Rassmussen (1996, 274–79) writes,

> Forms of nature are, in Luther's image, the 'masks' of God (*lavae dei*). . . . Nature is God's disguise. Nature is not God, but the source of the signs, the metaphors, the symbols of the *deus absconditus* (the hidden God). Nature is how and where the hidden God is revealed (*deus revelatus*). Here, in 'the majesty of matter,' we know God in the only way we, as finite creatures, can. Rain or a fruit tree or a child at the breast is a disguise of God's. None is God, but all are an epiphanic presence of God's presence. As with the grain, God is wholly present in them, and they wholly in God, but they do not exhaust the Inexhaustible One.

10. The non-reflective life of animals is not something toward which we should strive, according to Kierkegaard. In *The Sickness Unto Death*, Anti-Climacus associates "the crowd" with "what Aristotle calls the animal category" (SUD 118/SKS 11:230) and says that facing the possibility of despair because "he is spirit . . . is man's superiority over the animal" (SUD 15/ SKS 11:131).

Conclusion

*Consequences of Ethical Silence:
Teaching, Freedom, and Responsibility*

Ethical silence contributes to the fulfillment of both of the second ethics' imperatives to imitate Christ and to love the neighbor. The way in which silence fulfills these imperatives furthermore reveals the existence of three layers of silence within the second ethics. The first layer is religious silence, or the silence of inwardness, that lies at the foundation of the second ethics. The second layer of silence is the kind that is associates, in a general sense, with action. This silence purposefully stops words in order to set the "fundamental tone" (FSE 49/SKS 13:75) for action. The third layer refers to the silence that is connected to concealing what could be said in order to prevent boasting and chatter. This type of silence includes the purposeful concealment of the self and neighbor when done as an expression of love toward the neighbor (i.e., through opposing preference and endorsing equality). Several interpretative consequences come from the recognition of these three layers of ethical silence.

The third layer of silence, which refers to particular instantiations of silence that fulfill the imperative to love the neighbor, clearly shows that Kierkegaard believes that silence can be ethically appropriate. In *Fear and Trembling*, de silentio writes that "ethics demands disclosure" and requires that the ethical agent "expresses the universal" (FT 87/SKS 4:177). De silentio contends that by remaining silent, the ethical agent "takes a responsibility upon himself as the single individual" (FT 87/SKS 4:177) and subsequently falls short of the ethical by disregarding the claims of the universal. Of course, de silentio's interpretation of the ethical is consistent with what Kierkegaard calls the first ethics, an ethics in which there could not be a conceivable situation when silence would be justifiable. In sharp contrast to the first ethics which prioritizes universal disclosure, Kierkegaard offers his second ethics which subordinates the demand for universal disclosure under the demand to follow its given imperatives. The third layer of silence is composed of the examples of silence which prevent complete disclosure through purposeful concealment, but are nevertheless ethically appropriate since they serve to fulfill the second ethics' imperatives.

The ethical appropriateness of particular instantiations of silence within the second ethics shows that, for Kierkegaard, silence, in its own right, is morally neutral. What is meant here by silence's neutrality is that silence is neither intrinsically good nor bad. Rather, Kierkegaard's position appears to be that silence's ethical value is determined by context and how it is used in that context. As he writes, "A silence can have many characteristics tending toward good or evil. . . ." (TM 80/SKS 14:218). It is *how* silence is actually put into practice that establishes whether silence is "good or evil." One could also make a similar claim in the case of language; language does not have any inherent value for Kierkegaard, but instead language's value depends on how it is used. For example, using language to boast would be an instance of self-love and therefore would be unethical. However, using language to praise love is an act of love (WL 359/SKS 9:353), and thus is ethical. Shin Ohara (1967a, 243) makes this point in "Kierkegaard on Ethics and Language:" "Linguistic expression, by itself, is neither ethical nor unethical, for it remains neutral until it effects the ethical-religious reality. Linguistic expression per se remains neutral; only the individual commitment changes the significance of the expression." The ethical value of language or silence, then, is measured in terms of its compatibility with the second ethics' imperatives. When used sagaciously, silence is ethically unacceptable; when used to express love, silence is ethically appropriate. Therefore, the concept of silence possesses no particular ethical value, but the practice of silence does.

The assertion of silence's ethical neutrality shows a fundamental break between the first and second ethics caused by what Bernard Williams (1986, 197) calls the "tension . . . between reflection and practice." In Kierkegaard's second ethics, emphasis is placed on practice and action in opposition to reflection and conceptualization. For Kierkegaard, the mere concept of silence is ethically empty. The practice of silence is another matter, since an actual instantiation of silence reflects a motivation wherein its ethical value lies. Recall Mark Taylor's (1981, 180) statement that the "ethicist believes all forms of silence to be deceptive and deceitful" discussed in chapter 1; it is clear now that this only applies to the first ethics, but not to the second ethics.

Silence not only serves to reveal the distinction between concept and practice with regard to their ethical value, but silence is also inextricably linked with practice itself. This is what is meant by the second layer of silence. The second layer refers to the silence that is a condition for action, "... authentic intensive actions spring from an individual and from silence" (JP 4:100/SKS 24:212).

TEACHING ETHICS

The disjunction between reflection and practice extends to Kierkegaard's views on the issue of teaching ethics. Kierkegaard presents the problem the following way:

> It is unconditionally true of the ethical that it cannot be taught. The instructive lecture deals with an object—and ethically there simply is no object.... There is discussion *about* this object. But the lecture itself does not existentially [*existentielt*] express that the teacher exists [*existerer*] in it, nor does it occasion the listeners to exist in it. (JP 1:301/Pap. VIII-2 B 88)

For Kierkegaard, the correct way to teach ethics would involve the submersion of the teacher and the student into the actual activity of ethics. An "instructive lecture" cannot do this because it treats ethics as an "object" of knowledge which can be communicated through language. By using language, the teacher of ethics limits the scope of ethics to the realm of the possible, reduces it to "the medium of the imagination" (JP 1:286/Pap. VIII-2 B 85). But to do this reflects a "confusion" (JP 1:286/Pap. VIII-2 B 85) about ethics since authentic ethics is solely concerned with actuality, not possibility. For Kierkegaard, ethics pertains to the actual living of one's life and in following the constant motion of life, it always eludes reflective thought's grasp.

The problem of teaching ethics is resolved by silence, since it is in silence that the real work of ethics takes place. Kierkegaard's paradigmatic teachers, the lily of the field and the bird of the air "are what they teach, themselves express what they as teachers are teaching" (WA 38/SKS 11:42). The lesson they teach is silence: "From the lily and the bird as teachers, let us learn *silence*, or learn to be *silent*" (WA 10/SKS 11:16). The silence taught by the bird and lily is the "first condition for truly being able to obey ... God, who around you and within you speaks to you through silence" (WA 24–5/SKS 11:31). Obedience requires not only religious silence (the first layer of silence), the necessary silence of faith, but also the ethical silence of the second ethics which prioritizes actions over words (the second layer of ethical silence).

The silent teaching of ethics, in the way that Kierkegaard envisions, is strenuous for both the teacher and student. The teacher is to present a double-reflection and/or reduplicate (see chapter 3) in the teaching. In reduplication, the teacher is to be an "existing ethicist" (JP 1:269/Pap. VIII-2 B 81). The student of ethics is also required to venture into actuality, a venture that is not without effort and the potential for failure. Recall the ethics lesson as a swimming lesson: "As far as 'actuality' is concerned, almost all men have a kind of fear of water. They want the teacher to be related to them as the swimming instructor who in a safe and 'quiet hour' explains the motions of swimming to them; but when we says: Let us now dive in, they say: No thanks" (JP 1:287/Pap. VIII-2 B 85). The teaching and learning of ethics necessitates a "dive" into actuality and correspondingly a "dive" into silence. The teacher and student no longer engage over explanations of the motions of ethics, but are to silently engage in the motions themselves. This is true for the teacher, who is to silently reduplicate the lesson; "all instruction ends in a kind of silence; for when I existentially express it, it is not necessary for my speaking to be audible" (JP 1:286/Pap. VIII-2 B 85). It is also true for the student who is not to *speak about* what is required by the ethical, but is to do the actions that fulfill the requirements.[1] Kierkegaard writes, "The ethical and the ethical-religious have to be communicated existentially and in the direction of the existential" (JP 1:301/Pap. VIII-B 88).

ETHICAL FREEDOM

Kierkegaard's prioritization of practice over reflection also draws out interesting conclusions about freedom. It was stated above that the concept of silence is ethically empty, but that the actual use of silence can have ethical value. The motivation for using silence, whether it is used sagaciously or to express love for the neighbor, determines this value. Therefore, the second ethics is non-consequentialist, in that it does not attribute moral value to the outcomes of actions, but evaluates the motivations that inspire actions. For Kierkegaard, the ethical realm does not describe a simple linear relation between action and a singular ethical consequence, but consists of ethical motives that give rise to a variety of possible outcomes. Kierkegaard's non-consequentialism and non-determinism produce a radical freedom in his ethics. While consequentialist and determinist theories focus on the outward, visible, and predictable consequences of actions, Kierkegaard's position reverses the direction of focus so that the ethical emphasis is placed on the inward and private motivations of the subject who is not guaranteed a formulaic outcome. The ethical agent is therefore free from both the judgment of the universal, and the agent is also free in the sense that their actions are not determined by some invisible force, but rather are chosen. The second ethics assumes the agent's freedom *from* the universal which results in their freedom *to* choose. Both of these aspects of ethical freedom are connected to silence.

Levinas (1998, 28) writes,

> The great value of the Kierkegaardian notion of existence, with its deeply protestant protest against systems in general, is that it saw an impossibility within the very *capacity to speak* that was the achievement of totalizing thought. It descried within this discourse a faraway impossibility of discourse—the shadow of the evening hidden in the light of the midday sun. Behind the philosophy of totality which assuages the tension (possibly a sublime thirst for salvation) of subjective egoism it foresaw the end of philosophy, and how it would lead to a political totalitarianism in which we would cease to be the source of our own language and become mere reflections of an impersonal logos, or roles enacted by anonymous figures.

The "impossibility within the very capacity to speak" is the impossibility of congruence between language and actuality, the realm of the second ethics. For Kierkegaard, language is the medium of the "system" which ineffectually attempts to contain actuality and offer it up in its limited and distorted form. The political consequences of systems, whether they are totalitarianism or more subtle modes of oppression, yield unfreedom. Silence, on the other hand, operates to undermine such systems by denying "totalizing thought" and by preserving the religious and ethical choice for the individual alone. Kierkegaard associates the individual's silence with both freedom and originality:

> Silence is inward deepening and the road by which an originality is gained that is more than a substitute for the originality of genius. . . . By holding firm to a definite life-impression, a definite single thought, in absolutely silent inwardness, by not wanting to open the slightest communication with any other person (by which one slyly obtains the relative and comparative criterion, the criterion of mediocrity), anyone, provided he is not on the way to losing his mind (since there undeniably is this danger), will *acquire originality*. This is the road of freedom and of self-consciousness and of disciplined passion. . . . The idea of silence, the whole view of silence as inwardness, is the road of inward deepening to the highest for every human being, whether or not he is originally a genius. (BA 280/Pap. VII-2 B 235)

Originality, acquired through the silence of inward deepening, is not an ethical virtue within the first ethics because it contradicts universality, but is for Kierkegaard "the highest for every human being." The freedom produced from silence is freedom from the comparison and mediocrity of the universal. On this point, the break between Kierkegaard's philosophy and Enlightenment philosophies is clear. In *Dialectic of Enlightenment*, Horkheimer and Adorno (2002, 1) write, "Enlightenment, understood in the widest sense as the advance of thought, has always aimed at liberating human beings from fear and installing them as masters." For thinkers like Kant and Hegel, it is the universal nature of rationality that provide liberation; everyone has equal access to ethical truths and experiences freedom by following the dictates of reason instead of the dictates of political or religious authorities. However, for Kierkegaard, rationality proves to be just as confining as the power structures the Enlightenment sought to dethrone. For Kierkegaard, true freedom means the ability to make choices about things beyond reason's limited scope, such as ethical and religious decisions, because there can be no comprehensive ethical or religious formula or system that could account for the richness of actuality and human experience.

Although Kierkegaard's vision of freedom means that one's ethical decisions are no longer completely determined by reason nor are they subject to universal judgment, it would seem that this freedom also entails a loss of ethical authority. MacIntyre (1984, 39) describes Kierkegaard's *Either/Or* as being the outcome of the Enlightenment's ultimate failure, and this outcome is "disconcerting, even shocking:"

> What I earlier picked out as the distinctively modern standpoint was of course that which envisages moral debate in terms of a confrontation between incompatible and incommensurable moral premises and moral commitment as the expression of a criterionless choice between such premises, a type of choice for which no rational justification can be given. This element of arbitrariness in our moral culture was presented as a philosophical discovery—indeed as a discovery of a disconcerting, even shocking, kind—long before it became a commonplace of everyday discourse. Indeed that discovery was first presented precisely with the intention of shocking the participants in everyday moral discourse in a book which is at once the outcome and the epitaph of the Enlightenment's systematic attempt to discover a rational justification for morality. The book is Kierkegaard's *Enter-Eller*....

The scandal here is, of course, Kierkegaard's uncovering of the passionate, faithful decision that rests at the bottom of all moral commitment, a decision that is private, not public—a decision made in silence. Kierkegaard calls into question the artificial construct philosophy was building in the name of rationality that obscures the foundational choice to accept or reject the ethical. Along with Kierkegaard's "philosophical discovery" comes a perceived vacuum; if the standard bearers of authority (the king, the church, or reason) are no longer the ethical judges, then one wonders who or what is to assign ethical value to motivations and actions. This question is ultimately a question about ethical responsibility.

ETHICAL RESPONSIBILITY

As in the case of ethical freedom, silence also elucidates Kierkegaard's interpretation of ethical responsibility. For Kierkegaard, true ethical responsibility begins with religious silence, the first layer of silence in the second ethics. In *Concept of Anxiety*, Kierkegaard explicitly defines the second ethics as a religious, or "dogmatic," ethics that "has its ideality in the penetrating consciousness of actuality, of the actuality of sin" (CA 20/SKS 4:328). The positing of sin differentiates the second ethics from the first. The moral agent of the second ethics no longer finds ultimate judgment for their actions in the world (through the judgment of society or one's own rationality), but is related to God under the condition of obedience. The agent enters into this relationship with God in silence, the religious silence that reflects the ineffable nature of the connection between the individual and God. This is the silence associated with the "decisive choice" to have religious faith, which amounts to the choice to accept the authority of the imperatives of the second ethics.

Within the first ethics, language, as the medium of disclosure, serves as the indicator of the agent's ethicality. By revealing one's ethical motivations in language, ethical judgment becomes a public matter thereby making the community of rational agents the supreme judges. Yet Kierkegaard's concern is that such disclosure would not necessarily guarantee one's ethicality. It is possible, Kierkegaard thinks, that one could live their whole life under the mask of the ethical (for example, by acting upon reason and disclosing their motivations to others), yet could be in reality wholly unethical. For Kierkegaard, the problem with the first ethics and its reliance on language is that it makes the ethical subject to outwardness, to mere appearance, a talking *about* *x*, rather than a *doing or being x*. In contrast, the second ethics requires that the individual submerge under the appearance to the deeper recesses of one's own being and become truthful before self and God.

> It is certain that ordinarily a person acts more sensibly, shows more energy, apparently more self-control, when others are watching him than when he believes himself unobserved. But the question is whether this sensibleness, this energy, this self-control are in truth, or whether through the persistence of his attention in the untruth of appearance they do not easily light the inconstant flame of double-mindedness in his soul. Everyone who when before himself is not more ashamed than he is before others will, if he is placed in a difficult position and is sorely tried in life, end up becoming a slave of people in one way or another. What is it to be more ashamed before others than before oneself but to be more ashamed of seeming than of being? Indeed, conversely, a person ought to be more ashamed of being than of seeming; otherwise he cannot will one thing in truth, since in his wooing deference to appearance he only covets the changing semblance and its reflection in public favor. (UDVS 53/SKS 8:164)

The second ethics is Kierkegaard's name for an ethics that prioritizes responsibility to self and God over responsibility to the world. The particular role that silence plays is one of retaining responsibility within the self; "for by maintaining silence, a person is thrown wholly upon himself" (SUD 34/SKS

11:151). Derrida (1995, 58–59) articulates this connection between silence and responsibility: "One often thinks that responsibility consists of acting and signing in one's name . . . but as soon as one speaks, as soon as one enters the medium of language, one loses that very singularity." For Kierkegaard, silence is the truest test of ethical mettle, since by keeping silent the individual "leaves no outward trace" (SUD 34/SKS 11:151) so that there is no temptation to fall into the universal and its judgment. The strenuousness of the second ethics is not the strenuousness of keeping up ethical appearances, but the real strenuousness of being ethical.

Since ethical freedom consists in the breaking away from the authority of rationality and the world, and ethical responsibility resides completely with the single individual in obedience to God, Kierkegaard's ethics is, as he himself describes it, "an ethical stance despite the world."

> It is doubtful, then, that the age will be saved by the idea of sociality, of association. On the contrary, this idea is the skepticism necessary for the proper development of individuality, inasmuch as every individual either is lost or, disciplined by the abstraction, finds himself religiously. In our age the principle of association (which at best can have validity with respect to material interest) is not affirmative but negative; it is an evasion, a dissipation, an illusion, whose dialectic is as follows: as it strengthens individuals, it vitiates them; it strengthens by numbers, by sticking together, but from the ethical point of view this is a weakening. Not until the single individual has established an ethical stance despite the whole world, not until then can there be any question of genuinely uniting; otherwise it gets to be a union of people who separately are weak, a union as unbeautiful and depraved as a child-marriage. (TA 106/SKS 8:101)

It first appears that an "ethical stance despite the world" would be impossible since ethics concerns the individual's relations with others in the world and ethical actions take place in the world. However, Kierkegaard's inclusion of silence into his second ethics reveals how such a stance can be assumed. His second ethics is not an ethics of the world, per se, but is an ethics of transcendence. The individual is to act in the world, but their actions are not to be ultimately judged according to the world's standards. Rather, ethical value is determined by the dual-judge: the self and God. This is not to say, as many of Kierkegaard's critics have done, that Kierkegaard advocates a rejection of the world or human relationships, but rather Kierkegaard connects the second ethics to a particular sort of maturity in and with the world that can only be achieved by the "single individual." In *The Point of View*, Kierkegaard writes "to me . . . as a thinker, this matter of the single individual is the most decisive" (PV 114/SKS 16:94). While Kierkegaard argues that his age treats the "single individual" as a "triviality" (PV 114/SKS 16:94), his entire work is concerned with the maturation, the "upbringing," of the "single individual." The essence of this maturation is the shift from merely talking to actual doing, from ethical appearance to ethical silence. In describing the content of his later works, Kierkegaard writes, "The point in the whole thing is this: there is a zenith of Christianity in ethical rigorousness and this must at least by heard" (PV 201/SKS 22:149). For Kierkegaard, this address to the "single individual" is ultimately silent; it is heard in the silence that is "divinity's mutual understanding with the individual" (FT 88/SKS 4:178) and heard in the "silent and veracious eloquence of action" (PC 14/SKS 12:24).

NOTES

1. In addition to the swimming lesson example, Kierkegaard also uses the image of an army recruit and sergeant to show the difference between a communication of knowledge and a communication of capability:

> They tell a story about an army recruit who was supposed to learn to drill. The sergeant said to him: You, there, stand up straight. R.: Sure enough. Sgt.: Yes, and don't talk during the drill. R.: All right, I won't do that. Sgt.: No, you are not supposed to talk during the drill. R.: Yes, yes, if I just know it. The recruit's mistake is that he continually wants to transform an ability-communication into a communication of knowledge. But the mistake in the modern period is that the ethical and the ethical-religious have been taught, people have been given information about them. (JP 1:289/Pap. VIII-2 B 85)

Bibliography

Adorno, Theodor W. *Kierkegaard: Construction of the Aesthetic*. Minneapolis: University of Minnesota Press, 1989.
Aristotle. *A New Aristotle Reader*. Edited by J. L. Ackrill. Princeton: Princeton University Press, 1987.
Austin, J. L. "Performative Utterances" in *The Philosophy of Language: Second Edition*. Edited by A. P. Martinich. New York: Oxford University Press, 1990.
Axelson, Jens. *Dansk-engelsk Ordbog*. Copenhagen: Gyldendal, 1984.
Beiser, Frederick C. *The Fate of Reason: German Philosophy from Kant to Fichte*. Cambridge: Harvard University Press, 1987.
Berry, Wanda Warren. "The Silent Woman in Kierkegaard's Later Religious Writings" in *Feminist Interpretations of Søren Kierkegaard*. Edited by Céline Léon and Sylvia Walsh. University Park, Pennsylvania: The Pennsylvania State University Press, 1997.
Berthold, Daniel. "Kierkegaard's Seductions: The Ethics of Authorship," *MLN*. 120, 5. Baltimore: Johns Hopkins University Press. Dec 2005: 1004–1065.
———. *The Ethics of Authorship: Communication, Seduction, and Death in Hegel and Kierkegaard*. New York: Fordham University Press, 2011.
Betz, John R. *After Enlightenment: The Post-Secular Vision of J. G. Hamann*. Chichester, West Sussex: Wiley-Blackwell, 2008.
Bible: The New Oxford Annotated Bible, Revised Standard Version. Edited by Herbert G. May and Bruce M. Metzger. New York: Oxford University Press, 1962.
Blanchot, Maurice. *The Station Hill Blanchot Reader: Fiction and Literary Essays*. Edited by George Quasha. Barrytown. Translated by Lydia Davis, Paul Auster, and Robert Lamberton. NY: Station Hill Press, Inc., 1999.
Buben, Adam, Eleanor Helms, and Patrick Stokes, Eds. *The Kierkegaardian Mind*. New York: Routledge, 2019.
Cage, John. *Silence: Lectures and Writings by John Cage*. Hanover, NH: Wesleyan University Press, 1973.
Caputo, John. "Repetition and *Kinesis*: Kierkegaard on the Foundering of Metaphysics" in *Radical Hermeneutics: Repetition, Deconstruction, and the Hermeneutic Project*. Bloomington: Indiana University Press, 1988.
Compaijen, Rob, and Pieter Vos. "Ethical Reflection as Evasion." in *The Kierkegaardian Mind*. Edited by Adam Buben, Eleanor Helms, and Patrick Stokes. New York: Routledge, 2019.
Creegan, Charles L. *Wittgenstein and Kierkegaard: Religion, Individuality and Philosophical Method*. London: Routledge, 1989.
Crumbine, Nancy Jay. "On Silence." *Humanitas*. Vol. 11. May 1975: 147–165.

Dauenhauer, Bernard P. *Silence: The Phenomenon and Its Ontological Significance.* Bloomington: Indiana University Press, 1980.
Davenport, John J., and Anthony Rudd, Eds. *Kierkegaard After MacIntyre: Essays on Freedom, Narrative, and Virtue.* Chicago: Open Court, 2001.
Derrida, Jacques. *The Gift of Death.* Translated by David Wills. Chicago: The University of Chicago Press, 1995.
Dooley, Mark. *The Politics of Exodus: Kierkegaard's Ethics of Responsibility.* New York: Forham University Press, 2001.
Evans, C. Stephen. *Kierkegaard's Ethic of Love: Divine Commands and Moral Obligations.* New York: Oxford University Press, 2004.
Fenves, Peter. *Chatter: Language and History in Kierkegaard.* Stanford: Stanford University Press, 1993.
Ferreira, M. Jamie. *Love's Grateful Striving: A Commentary on Kierkegaard's Works of Love.* New York: Oxford University Press, 2001.
Fremstedal, Roe. "Kierkegaard's Views on Normative Ethics, Moral Agency, and Metaethics," in *A Companion to Kierkegaard*, 113–124. Edited by Jon Stewart. Chichester, West Sussex: Wiley Blackwell, 2015.
Garff, Joakim. "Rereading Oneself." *Søren Kierkegaard Newsletter.* Edited by Gordon D. Marino, Northfield, MN: St. Olaf College. Number 38. July 1999: 9–14.
Goethe, Johann Wolfgang Von. *Goethe's Faust: The Prologues and Part I.* Translated by Bayard Taylor. New York: Collier Books, 1963.
Green, Ronald. "Developing *Fear and Trembling*" in *The Cambridge Companion to Kierkegaard.* Edited by Alastair Hannay and Gordon D. Marino. Cambridge: Cambridge University Press, 1998.

———. *Kierkegaard and Kant: The Hidden Debt.* Albany: State University of New York Press, 1992.

Grice, H. P., "Logic and Conversation" in *The Philosophy of Language. Second Edition.* Edited by A. P. Martinich. New York: Oxford University Press, 1990.
Griffith-Dickson, Gwen. *Johann Georg Hamann's Relational Metacriticism.* New York: Walter de Gruyter, 1995.
Grøn, Arne. *The Concept of Anxiety in Søren Kierkegaard.* Translated by Jeanette B. L. Knox. Macon, GA: Mercer University Press, 2008.
Hamann, Johann Georg. *Hamann's Socratic Memorabilia: A Translation and Commentary.* Translated by James C. O'Flaherty. Baltimore: The Johns Hopkins Press, 1967.

———. *Writings on Philosophy and Language.* Translated by Kenneth Haynes. New York: Cambridge University Press, 2007.

Hannay, Alastair. *Kierkegaard.* New York: Routledge, 1991

———. and Gordon D. Marino., eds. *The Cambridge Companion to Kierkegaard.* New York: Cambridge University Press, 1998.

Hay, Sergia. "Hamann: Sharing Style and Thesis: Kierkegaard's Appropriation of Hamann's Work." in *Kierkegaard and His German Contemporaries: Tome III: Literature and Aesthetics.* Edited by Jon Stewart. Burlington, VT: Ashgate Publishing Limited, 2008.
Hegel, G. W. F. *Phänomenologie des Geistes.* Hamburg: Felix Meiner Verlag, 1988.

———. *Phenomenology of Spirit.* Translated by A. V. Miller. New York: Oxford University Press,1977.

———. *Elements of the Philosophy of Right.* Edited by Allen W. Wood. Translated by H. B. Nisbet. Cambridge: Cambridge University Press, 1991.

Heidegger, Martin. *Poetry, Language, Thought.* Translated by Albert Hofstadter. New York: Harper & Row, Publishers, 1971.
Holmer, Paul L. *The Paul L. Holmer Papers. Vol 1: On Kierkegaard and the Truth.* Edited by David J. Gouwens and Lee C. Barrett III. Eugene, OR: Cascade Books, 2012.

———."Kierkegaard and Religious Propositions." *The Journal of Religion* XXXV. 3 (1955): 135–146.

Horkheimer, Max, and Theodor W. Adorno. *Dialectic of Enlightenment: Philosophical Fragments.* Edited by Gunzelin Schmid Noerr. Translated by Edmund Jephcott. Stanford, California: Stanford University Press, 2002.

Houe, Poul, et al., eds. *Anthropology and Authority: Essays on Søren Kierkegaard*. Amsterdam: Rodopi, 2000.
Hough, Sheridan. *Kierkegaard's Dancing Tax Collector: Faith, Finitude, and Silence*. Oxford: Oxford University Press, 2015.
Jenson, Matt. *The Gravity of Sin: Augustine, Luther, and Barth on* Homo Incurvatus in Se. London: T&T Clark, 2006
Kafka, Franz. *The Complete Stories*. Edited by Nahum N. Glatzer. New York: Schocken Books, 1971.
Kant, Immanuel. *Critique of Pure Reason*. Translated by Norman Kemp Smith. New York: St. Martin's Press, 1929.
———. *Groundwork of the Metaphysic of Morals*. Translated by H. J. Patton. New York: Harper Torchbooks, 1964.
———. *On the Old Saw: That May be Right in Theory But It Won't Work in Practice*. Translated by E. B. Ashton. Philadelphia: University of Pennsylvania Press, 1974.
———. "An Answer to the Question: What Is Enlightenment?" in *What Is Enlightenment? Eighteenth-Century Answers and Twentieth-Century Questions*. Edited and translated by James Schmidt. Berkeley: University of California Press, 1996. pp. 58–64.
Kierkegaard, Søren. *The Book on Adler*. Edited and translated by Howard V. Hong and Edna H. Hong. Princeton: Princeton University Press, 1998.
———. *Christian Discourses/The Crisis and a Crisis in the Life of an Actress*. Edited and translated by Howard V. Hong and Edna H. Hong. Princeton: Princeton University Press, 1997.
———. *Concluding Unscientific Postscript to Philosophical Fragments*. Edited and translated by Howard V. Hong and Edna H. Hong. Princeton: Princeton University Press, 1992.
———. *The Concept of Anxiety: A Simple Psychologically Orienting Deliberation on the Dogmatic Issue of Hereditary Sin*. Edited and translated by Reidar Thomte. Princeton: Princeton University Press, 1980.
———. *The Concept of Irony with Continual Reference to Socrates/ Notes of Schelling's Berlin Lectures*. Edited and translated by Howard V. Hong and Edna H. Hong. Princeton: Princeton University Press, 1989.
———. *Eighteen Upbuilding Discourses*. Edited and translated by Howard V. Hong and Edna H. Hong. Princeton: Princeton University Press, 1990.
———. *Either/Or*. Edited and translated by Howard V. Hong and Edna H. Hong. Princeton: Princeton University Press, 1987.
———. *Fear and Trembling/Repetition*. Edited and translated by Howard V. Hong and Edna H. Hong. Princeton: Princeton University Press, 1983.
———. *For Self-Examination/Judge for Yourself!*. Edited and translated by. Howard V. Hong and Edna H. Hong. Princeton: Princeton University Press, 1990.
———. *Kierkegaard's Journals and Notebooks: Vols. 1–11*. Edited and translated by Niels Jørgen Cappelørn, Alastair Hannay, David Kangas, Bruce H. Kirmmse, George Pattison, Vanessa Rumble, and K. Brian Söderquist. Princeton: Princeton University Press, 2007–2019.
———. *The Moment and Late Writings*. Edited and translated by Howard V. Hong and Edna H. Hong. Princeton: Princeton University Press, 1998.
———. *Philosophical Fragments/Johannes Climacus*. Edited and translated by Howard V. Hong and Edna H. Hong. Princeton: Princeton University Press, 1985.
———. *The Point of View*. Edited and translated by Howard V. Hong and Edna H. Hong. Princeton: Princeton University Press, 1998.
———. *Practice in Christianity*. Edited and translated by Howard V. Hong and Edna H. Hong. Princeton: Princeton University Press, 1991.
———. *Samlede værker*. Bind 1–19. Copenhagen: Gyldendalske Boghandel, 1962.
———. *The Sickness Unto Death: A Christian Psychological Exposition for Upbuilding and Awakening*. Edited and translated by Howard V. Hong and Edna H. Hong. Princeton: Princeton University Press, 1980.

———. *Søren Kierkegaard's Journals and Papers:* 7 vols. Edited and translated by Howard Hong and Edna Hong, assisted by Gregor Malantschuck. Bloomington: Indiana University Press, vol. 1: 1967; vol. 2: 1970; vols. 3 and 4: 1975; vols. 5–7:1978.
———. *Søren Kierkegaards Skrifter.* Edited by Niels Jørgen Cappelørn, Joakim Garff, Jette Knudsen, Johnny Kondrup, and Alastair McKinnon. Copenhagen: Gads Forlag, 1997–2012.
———. *Stages on Life's Way.* Edited and translated by Howard V. Hong and Edna H. Hong. Princeton: Princeton University Press, 1988.
———. *Three Discourses on Imagined Occasions.* Edited and translated by Howard V. Hong and Edna H. Hong. Princeton: Princeton University Press, 1993.
———. *Two Ages.* Edited and translated by Howard V. Hong and Edna H. Hong. Princeton University Press, 1978.
———. *Upbuilding Discourses in Various Spirits.* Edited and translated by Howard V. Hong and Edna H. Hong. Princeton: Princeton University Press, 1993.
———. *Without Authority.* Edited and translated by Howard V. Hong and Edna H. Hong. Princeton: Princeton University Press, 1997.
———. *Works of Love.* Edited and translated by Howard V. Hong and Edna H. Hong. Princeton: Princeton University Press, 1995.
Kingwell, Mark. "'We Shall Look into it Tomorrow': Kierkegaard and the Art of Procrastination." *Toronto Journal of Theology.* University of Toronto Press. 29(2). Fall 2013: 211–226.
Kirmmse, Bruce H. *Kierkegaard in Golden Age Denmark.* Bloomington: Indiana University Press, 1990.
Léon, Céline and Walsh, Sylvia., eds. *Feminist Interpretations of Søren Kierkegaard.* University Park, Pennsylvania: The Pennsylvania State University Press, 1997.
Levinas, Emmanuel. "Existence and Ethics" in *Kierkegaard: A Critical Reader.* Edited by Jonathan Rée and Jane Chamberlain. Oxford: Blackwell Publishers Ltd., 1998.
Lippitt, John. "Beyond Worry? On Learning Humility from the Lilies and the Birds." in *The Kierkegaardian Mind.* Edited by Adam Buben, Eleanor Helms, and Patrick Stokes. New York: Routledge, 2019.
———. *Kierkegaard and the Problem of Self-Love.* New York: Cambridge University Press, 2013.
MacCulloch, Diarmaid. *Silence: A Christian History.* New York: Penguin, 2013.
MacIntyre, Alasdair. *After Virtue: A Study in Moral Theory.* Notre Dame, Indiana: University of Notre Dame Press, 1984.
Mahn, Jason A. *Fortunate Fallibility: Kierkegaard and the Power of Sin.* New York: Oxford University Press, 2011.
Manheimer, Ronald J. *Kierkegaard as Educator.* Berkeley: University of California Press, 1977.
Marino, Gordon. "The Place of Reason in Kierkegaard's Ethics" in *Kierkegaard After MacIntyre: Essays on Freedom, Narrative, and Virtue.* Edited by John J. Davenport and Anthony Rudd. Chicago: Open Court, 2001.
McGowan, Mary Kate. *Just Words: On Speech and Hidden Harm.* New York: Oxford University Press, 2019.
Mooney, Edward F. *On Søren Kierkegaard: Dialogue, Polemics, Lost Intimacy, and Time,* Burlington, VT: Ashgate Publishing Ltd., 2007.
———. *Knights of Faith and Resignation: Reading Kierkegaard's Fear and Trembling.* Albany: State University of New York Press, 1991.
Muller, Herbert J., "A Note on Methods of Analysis" in *The Limits of Language.* Edited by Walker Gibson. New York: Hill and Wang, 1962. pp. 29–34.
Nietzsche, Friedrich. *Basic Writings of Nietzsche.* Edited and translated by Walter Kaufmann. New York: The Modern Library, 1992.
Ohara, Shin. "Kierkegaard on Ethics and Language" in *Christianity and Culture,* III, June 1967: 241–269.
———. "Language and the Ethical in the Thought of Kierkegaard" in *Journal of Aoyama Gakuin Woman's Junior College.* No. 21. Tokyo: November, 1967: 1–37.
Pattison, George., ed. *Kierkegaard on Art and Communication.* New York: St. Martin's Press, Inc., 1992.

———. *The Philosophy of Kierkegaard*. Montreal and Kingston: McGill-Queen's University Press, 2005.
Pérez-Álverez, Eliseo. *A Vexing Gadfly: The Late Kierkegaard on Economic Matters*. Eugene, Oregon: Pickwick Publications, 2009.
Peters, John Durham. *Speaking into the Air: A History of the Idea of Communication*. Chicago: The University of Chicago Press, 1999.
Plato. *Complete Works*. Edited by John M. Cooper. Indianapolis: Hackett Publishing Company, 1997.
Podmore, Simon. "The Sacrifice of Silence: Fear and Trembling and the Secret of Faith." *International Journal of Systematic Theology*, vol. 14, no. 1, 2012: 70–90.
Poole, Roger. "The Unknown Kierkegaard: Twentieth-century Receptions" in *The Cambridge Companion to Kierkegaard*. Edited by Alastair Hannay and Gordon D. Marino. New York: Cambridge University Press, 1998.
Quinn, Philip L., "Kierkegaard's Christian Ethics" in *The Cambridge Companion to Kierkegaard*. Edited by Alastair Hannay and Gordon D. Marino. New York: Cambridge University Press, 1998.
Rassmussen, Larry L., *Earth Community/ Earth Ethics*. Geneva: WCC Publications, 1996.
Rocca, Ettore. "Kierkegaard's Second Aesthetics" in *Kierkegaard Studies, Yearbook 1999*. Edited by Niels Jørgen Cappelørn and Hermann Deuser. Berlin: Walter de Gruyter, 1999.
———. "Søren Kierkegaard and Silence" in *Anthropology and Authority: Essays on Søren Kierkegaard*. Edited by Poul Houe, Gordon D. Marino and Sven Hakon Rossel. Amsterdam: Rodopi, 2000.
Rudd, Anthony. *Kierkegaard and the Limits of the Ethical*. Oxford: Clarendon Press, 1993.
———. "Reason in Ethics: MacIntyre and Kierkegaard." in *Kierkegaard After MacIntyre: Essays on Freedom, Narrative, and Virtue*. Edited by John J. Davenport and Anthony Rudd. Chicago: Open Court, 2001.
Rumble, Vanessa. "Love and Difference: The Christian Ideal in Kierkegaard's Works of Love." in *The New Kierkegaard*. Edited by Elsbet Jegstrup. Bloomington: Indiana University Press, 2004.
Saez Tajafuerce, Begonya. "*Works of Love*: Modernity or Antiquity?" in *Kierkegaard Studies, Yearbook 1998*. Edited by Niels Jørgen Cappelørn and Hermann Deuser. Berlin: Walter de Gruyter, 1998.
Sartre, Jean Paul. *"What Is Literature?" and Other Essays*. Cambridge, MA: Harvard University Press, 1988.
Scarpi, Paolo. "The Eloquence of Silence: Aspects of a Power without Words" in *The Regions of Silence:Studies on the Difficulty of Communicating*. Edited by Maria Grazia Ciani. Amsterdam: J.C. Gieben, Publisher, 1987.
Schön, Alberto. "Silence in the Myth: Psychoanalytical Observations" in *The Regions of Silence: Studies on the Difficulty of Communicating*. Edited by Maria Grazia Ciani. Amsterdam: J.C. Gieben, Publisher, 1987.
Scollon, Ron. "The Machine Stops: Silence in the Metaphor of Malfunction" in *Perspectives on Silence*. Edited by Deborah Tannen and Muriel Saville-Troike. Norwood, NJ: Ablex, 1985.
Searle, John R. "What Is A Speech Act?" in *The Philosophy of Language: Second Edition*. Edited by A.P. Martinich. New York: Oxford University Press, 1990.
Shakespeare, Steven. "Significant Silences." in *Kierkegaard, Language, and the Reality of God*. New York: Routledge, 2018.
Søderquist, Anna Strelis. *Kierkegaard on Dialogical Education: Vulnerable Freedom*. Lanham, MD: Lexington Books, 2016.
Steiner, George. *Language and Silence: Essays on Language, Literature, and the Inhuman*. New York: Atheneum, 1967.
———. Introduction to *Fear and Trembling/Book on Adler* by Søren Kierkegaard. Translated by Walter Lowrie. New York: Everyman's Library Alfred A. Knopf, 1994.
Strawser, Michael. "Gifts of Silence from Kierkegaard and Derrida." *Soundings: An Interdisciplinary Journal*. Vol. 89. No. 1. University Park, Pennsylvania: Penn State University Press, 2006: 55–72.

Taylor, Mark C. "Sounds of Silence" in *Kierkegaard's "Fear and Trembling:" Critical Appraisals*. Edited by Robert L. Perkins. University, Alabama: The University of Alabama Press, 1981.

———. *Journeys to Selfhood: Hegel and Kierkegaard*. New York: Fordham University Press, 2000.

Tietjen, Mark A. *Kierkegaard, Communication, and Virtue: Authorship as Edification*. Bloomington: Indiana University Press, 2013.

Tillich, Paul. *The Courage to Be*. New Haven: Yale University Press, 1952.

Vlastos, Gregory. "Socratic Irony," in *Essays on the Philosophy of Socrates*. Edited by Hugh H. Benson. New York: Oxford University Press, 1992.

Walsh, Sylvia. "Reading Kierkegaard With Kierkegaard Against Garff." *Søren Kierkegaard Newsletter*. Edited by Marino, Gordon D., Northfield, MN: St. Olaf College. Number 38. July 1999: 4–8.

Westphal, Merold. *Becoming a Self: A Reading of Kierkegaard's Concluding Unscientific Postscript*. West Lafayette, IN: Purdue University Press, 1996.

———. "Kierkegaard and Hegel" in *The Cambridge Companion to Kierkegaard*. Edited by Alastair Hannay and Gordon D. Marino. New York: Cambridge University Press, 1998.

Williams, Bernard. *Ethics and the Limits of Philosophy*. Cambridge, MA: Harvard University Press, 1986.

Wittgenstein, Ludwig. *Culture and Value*. Translated by Peter Winch. Chicago: The University of Chicago Press, 1980.

———. *Lectures and Conversations on Aesthetics, Psychology and Religious Belief*. Edited by Cyril Barrett. Berkeley: University of California Press, 1966.

———. "Wittgenstein's Lecture on Ethics." *Philosophical Review*. 1965: 3–13.

Zijlstra, Onno. *Language, Image, and Silence: Kierkegaard and Wittgenstein on Ethics and Aesthetics*. Bern: Peter Lang, 2006.

Index

Abraham, 6, 24, 34, 68
action, 1, 3, 51–53, 58–59, 65, 66, 67–68, 89, 90, 92, 97
Adler, Adolph Peter, 87n7
Adorno, Theodor W., 26, 29n14, 93
Agamemnon, 8
animals, 3, 83, 84–85, 86n5, 87n10
Aristotle, 14, 18, 87n10
Austin, J. L., 59n3

Beiser, Frederick, 80
Berens, Johann Christoph, 79, 80, 86n2
Betz, John, 81–82, 86n2
Blanchot, Maurice, 50

Cage, John, 52
cannibals, 37
Caputo, John, 35
chatter, 39, 58, 74, 89
children, 46n5, 73, 75n6
Christ, 44, 47n11; contemporaneity with, 62; imitation of, 2, 3, 24–25, 26, 27, 29n13, 29n15, 35, 36, 61–68, 89; as *logos*, 66; as paradox, 63; as truth, 66
communication: of capability, 3, 40, 41, 42–44, 66, 77, 97n1; Kierkegaard's lectures on, 2, 39–42, 46n6; of knowledge, 3, 39, 40, 41–42, 77, 97n1
Compaijen, Rob, 22, 37
comparison, 2, 72, 93

concealment, 7, 8, 9, 53, 57, 70, 74, 75n3, 75n9, 79–80, 89–90
Crumbine, Nancy Jay, 5

Dauenhauer, Bernard P., 59n1
Derrida, Jacques, 35, 96
de silentio, Johannes, 8, 35, 53, 55, 89
despair, 54–55, 87n10
dogmatics, 19, 25
dogmatism, 16–17, 21
Don Juan, 7
double-mindedness, 68

education, 40, 42, 73, 91–92. *See also* maieutic method; Socrates
established order, 63, 66
ethics: activity of, 31, 37–44; description of, 31, 45; evasion of, 22, 36, 37–39, 42, 66–67; first, 2, 13–18, 21, 34, 89, 90, 93, 95; second, 2, 18–27, 32–37, 35, 36, 61, 90, 91, 92, 93, 95, 96; striving for, 25–26, 36
equality, 2, 69, 71–72, 73, 74, 89
equalizing, 2, 3, 73, 74
Evans, C. Stephen, 10n2

Fenves, Peter, 51
freedom, 18, 92–94

Garff, Joakim, 46n10
Goethe, Johann Wolfgang, 17, 28n3

grace, 25–26, 38
Green, Roland, 11n4, 28n4
Grice, H. Paul, 32
Griffith-Dickson, Gwen, 80, 82
Grøn, Arne, 6, 10

Hamann, Johann, 29n11, 34, 46n4, 78–83, 86n1, 86n2, 86n3
happiness, 8, 64
Hegel, Georg Wilhelm Friedrich, 13, 14, 16–17, 28n3, 34, 63, 93
Heidegger, Martin, 45n1
Hobbes, Thomas, 55
Holmer, Paul, 5
Horkheimer, Max, 93
Hough, Sheridan, 6
humility, 10, 64, 70–71, 74, 75n4, 80, 82, 83
humor, 80–81
hypocrisy, 31, 32, 37, 42, 83, 85

imperatives: of second ethics, 22–27, 26, 27, 62, 74–75, 89–90. *See also* Kant, categorical imperative; ethics, second
inclosing reserve, 54
inwardness, 1, 3, 7, 33–34, 45n3, 56, 63–64, 65, 89, 92, 93
irony, 31, 32, 81, 85

Jenson, Matt, 54
Job, 73

Kafka, Franz, 35, 46n5
Kant, Immanuel, 2, 8, 9, 13, 14–17, 18, 24, 28n2, 28n4, 29n9, 45n3, 79, 80, 81, 86n2, 93; categorical imperative of, 14, 15, 16, 17, 36
Kierkegaard, Søren: *The Book on Adler*, 93; *The Concept of Anxiety*, 14, 15, 18, 19, 28n8, 32, 36, 54, 82, 83, 95; *Concluding Unscientific Postscript*, 33, 45n3; *Either/Or*, 16, 57; *Fear and Trembling*, 54, 55, 89, 97; *For Self-Examination*, 1, 59, 62, 66, 67, 68, 75n1, 84, 85, 87n8, 89; *Journals and Papers*, 21, 26, 29n12, 32, 37, 38–39, 39–42, 46n7, 46n8, 47n11, 56, 57–58, 58, 59, 64–65, 69, 71, 77, 78, 84–85, 86, 86n4, 86n5, 87n7, 90, 91, 91–92,
97n1; *Kierkegaard's Journals and Notebooks*, 81; *"The Moment" and Late Writings*, 62, 90; *Philosophical Fragments* and *Johannes Climacus*, 37, 42; *The Point of View for My Work as an Author*, 2, 5, 25, 26, 32, 42, 96–97; *Practice in Christianity*, 20, 25, 26, 27, 29n13, 43–44, 45n3, 56–57, 58, 61, 62–64, 65, 66, 69, 86, 97; *The Sickness Unto Death*, 87n10, 95–96; *Two Ages*, 24, 56, 58, 58–59, 65, 96; *Upbuilding Discourses in Various Spirits*, 53, 67, 68, 70, 72–73, 75n3, 75n6, 95; *Without Authority*, 1, 59, 72, 75n6, 91; *Works of Love*, 22, 23, 24, 25, 27, 36, 69, 69–70, 70, 71–72, 73, 73–74, 75n4, 75n5, 90
Kingwell, Mark, 28n5
Kirmmse, Bruce, 28n1

language: depreciation of, 37, 38–39, 65; misuse of, 31, 32, 37–39, 84, 85–86; nature of, 31, 32–37; as negative, 50; use of, 31–32
Levinas, Emmanuel, 92–93
lily: and bird, 84, 87n6, 91; parable of, 72
logical positivism, 34
love, 10; Christian, 23–24; preferential, 23, 69–70, 70, 75n5, 89; of self, 2, 23, 69, 74, 90; Socratic, 81. *See also* neighbor, love of
Luther, Martin, 62, 87n9

MacIntyre, Alastair, 20, 21, 29n10, 94
Mahn, Jason, 28n7
maieutic method, 43, 44, 75n7. *See also* education; Socrates
Marino, Gordon, 29n10
McGowan, Mary Kate, 59n2
Mill, John Stuart, 59n2
Mooney, Edward F., 11n3
music, 7

Narcissus, 55
nature, 53, 73, 75n6, 84, 86, 86n4, 87n7, 87n8, 87n9
neighbor: as equal, 71–72; love of, 2, 3, 22, 25, 26, 35, 36, 69–75, 89, 92; meaning of, 23, 26, 27, 36, 69

non-human, 3, 77, 84–85. *See also* animals; lily

offense, 63, 64
Ohara, Shin, 31, 32–36, 45, 90

paradox, 9, 54, 55, 63, 65, 78, 81
Parmenides, 34
Pérez-Álvarez, Eliseo, 24
Plato, 18, 46n7, 52, 59n5, 59n6, 59n7, 78, 83
Podmore, Simon, 2
professors, 38
puzzles, 3, 43–44, 46n10, 56, 77, 78, 80. *See also* reflection, double; reduplication

Quinn, Philip L., 28n6

Rand, Ayn, 55
Rasmussen, Larry, 85, 87n9
rationality, 9, 94, 95, 96
reason, 15–17, 19–22, 29n9, 29n11, 68, 80, 82, 94. *See also* rationality
reduplication, 42, 44, 57–58, 77, 91
reflection, 22, 27, 31, 44; double, 43, 56–58, 77, 78, 80, 83, 91
relativism, 16–17
responsibility, 94–96
Rocca, Ettore, 2, 54
Rudd, Anthony, 17, 29n10

Saez Tajafuerce, Begonya, 25, 26–27, 29n14, 29n15
sagacity, 70–71, 71, 72, 75n8, 90, 92
Sartre, Jean Paul, 49, 50
Scarpi, Paolo, 50
Schön, Alberto, 67–68

Scollon, Ron, 49
Searle, John, 51
secrets. *See* concealment
silence: as communication, 50–52, 56–59; ethical uses of, 61–75; as fundamental tone, 1, 59, 68, 89; kinds of, 7; as negative, 49–50
sin, 54; hereditary, 19, 25; hiding neighbor's, 73–74
single individual, 6, 24, 63–64, 96
Socrates, 3, 40, 42, 46n7, 52, 59n5, 59n6, 59n7, 77–83, 86n3; as midwife, 42; Socratic ignorance, 77–80, 81–83. *See also* education; maieutic method
sophrosyne, 14
Shakespeare, Steven, 2
stages: aesthetic, 7; ethical, 8; of existence, 6–10; religious, 9
Steiner, George, 49–50, 50, 55
Strawser, Michael, 2

Taylor, Mark, 2, 6–10, 11n5, 70, 90
Tillich, Paul, 33

universal, the, 8, 11n4, 15–16, 34, 63, 89, 92, 93, 96

Vlastos, Gregory, 86
Vos, Pieter, 22, 37

Walsh, Sylvia, 46n10
Warren Barry, Wanda, 2, 87n6
will: God's, 37; weakness of, 18, 28n5
Williams, Bernard, 90
Wittgenstein, Ludwig, 45n2
worry, 72

Zijlstra, Onno, 2

About the Author

Sergia Hay is Associate Professor of Philosophy and Director of the Wild Hope Center for Vocation at Pacific Lutheran University. She studied at Wellesley College, Cambridge University, Luther Seminary, and Columbia University (Ph.D. 2003), and teaches courses in applied ethics and the history of philosophy. She also founded the South Puget Sound Chapter of the Society of Philosophers in America (SOPHIA), a public philosophy discussion group.

www.ingramcontent.com/pod-product-compliance
Lightning Source LLC
Chambersburg PA
CBHW050910300426
44111CB00010B/1468